MANAGING EMPLOYEE STRESS

SUPPORT YOUR STAFF BY PREVENTING OR REDUCING STRESS IN THE WORKPLACE WITH THIS STEP-BY-STEP GUIDE

LESLEY TOWNER

KOGAN PAGE

First published in 1998

Kogan Page Limited
120 Pentonville Road
London N1 9JN

© Lesley Towner, 1998

The right of Lesley Towner to be identified as the author of this work has been asserted by her in accordance with the Copyright, Designs and Patents Act 1988.

British Library Cataloguing in Publication Data

A CIP record for this book is available from the British Library.

ISBN 0 7494 2515 6

Typeset by BookEns Ltd, Royston, Herts.
Printed and bound in Great Britain by Clays Ltd, St Ives plc

Contents

Acknowledgements

I would particularly like to thank Joan Akrill, Maxine Jones and David Taylor for their valuable advice, and my family and friends for their continuing support and encouragement.

Introduction

Stress is not a new phenomenon. In fact, our response to stress is a relic from the Stone Age. What is new, however, is our greater recognition and awareness not only of its detrimental effects on us as individuals, but also of its negative effects in the workplace. In a highly competitive world, this matters.

Research has made great advances in our understanding in this field recently. Yet it is not necessary for managers to understand in depth the physiology and psychology of stress in order to appreciate its causes and effects in the workplace, or to take action to minimize these.

This guide is therefore a tour of the essential aspects of stress which managers need to know. It includes practical strategies and a simple stress inventory to provide over-worked managers with enough information to enable them to enhance their employees' mental wellbeing, to minimize the amount of stress experienced in the workplace, to increase productivity, and to help protect their employers against litigation.

While some 'experts' in the field of stress believe that all negative stress is personally inflicted through inadequate coping strategies, the theme of this guide is that although we can all do something to help ourselves when we are stressed, there is much that can be done and must be done by managers to minimize the stressors that exist within the workplace. Health and safety legislation places a responsibility on employers to take action to protect the health of their workers. This guide offers practical suggestions as to how this can be done with minimal cost or effort.

What is required from the manager is an open mind, an ability to think flexibly, and a willingness to change.

In writing this guide, some fundamental assumptions have been made:

about managers:

- Managers are busy people.
- They need information which is uncluttered and easy to access.
- They need only the basic information to get by.
- They need practical solutions to real problems.
- They need to look after themselves first and foremost.

about stress:

- Stress exists.
- Stress can affect anyone, whatever their level in the organization.
- The effects of stress are costly to an organization if ignored.
- The effects of stress are normally temporary if addressed early.
- Workplace stressors can be eliminated or reduced.
- People can recover fully from stress if supported.
- The amount of stress in a workplace is a barometer of the health of the organization. ✗

How to Use the Guide

This guide has been written in a logical, progressive order so that each chapter takes the manager a little further into understanding and dealing with stress in the workplace.

However, the guide can also be used as a support to a manager who already has some understanding of stress, but needs practical strategies to support this understanding.

The contents pages detail what each chapter covers, and each chapter itself concludes with a summary of the main points. Busy managers who want to respond urgently to stressed employees could therefore use either the contents pages or the summaries to locate the specific help they need.

Each chapter also concludes with some practical exercises to reinforce the main aspects of the chapter concerned. These could be used by managers on an individual basis, or they could become the focus of a group exercise or training session.

The Workplace Stress Inventory can stand by itself, and at the end of the inventory there are suggestions of how it can be used in the workplace.

Whichever way you choose to use the guide, you will find that it contributes to a greater understanding of your role as manager in relation to the stressed employee and provides you with practical solutions to sensitive issues.

Relax and enjoy it.

CHAPTER I
Why Stress Should Matter to the Employer

Even before we look at what stress is, how it is caused and how it affects people at work, we need to look at the reasons why employers cannot afford to ignore stress in their workplaces.

The reasons are essentially commercial ones. Employers are in the business of providing goods and services. The more efficiently and effectively this can be done, the greater the customer satisfaction, the greater the profit, the better the service, and the better the accountability where the public purse is concerned.

Employers and their managers may also be caring people who want the best for their staff and who are concerned about their staff's wellbeing within or outside the workplace. They will be aware that a stressed employee is not a happy, productive person, and they know that looking after their employees' wellbeing is good for business. But why is it?

Being a good employer

Being *thought of* as a good employer is good for business. The public who buys the products or uses the service looks more favourably on organizations which appear to care. When jobs

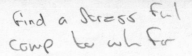

are advertised, potential employees make a judgement about whether they wish to work for the employer concerned. A poor reputation puts people off, which means that the choice of best person for the job is somewhat reduced. Judgements about products, services or employment opportunities are made on what people read in the papers, hearsay from friends and relatives, and the accounts of employees and ex-employees. The grapevine is a powerful force. The cost, for example, of an adverse industrial tribunal ruling is not limited to financial awards but to the knock-on effect in the market place.

Being a good employer is also good for business. Employees who feel that management cares, who benefit from the facilities or the policies or procedures which are designed to enhance their ability to work effectively, will be more committed, more motivated, and thus more effective (because they are more productive and efficient) than those who feel they are treated in a cavalier fashion by an employer who doesn't care. While the motivation to be a good employer may stem from an altruistic or principled stance, the benefits are also commercial.

We can look at the commercial aspect in further detail, concentrating on the financial costs of ignoring the impact of stress in the workplace.

The cost of stress in the workplace

Stress exists, whether we like it or not. It affects people in different ways, and if left untreated can create havoc in the workplace. The problem is that this havoc is wreaked below the surface. It is often hidden. But it exists and it is costly. Employers ignore it at their peril.

Some employers take the view that if stress comes from people's personal lives (and often it does) then it is not the responsibility of the employer. Quite right. But only up to a point. It is not their responsibility in the legal sense, but it is their commercial responsibility.

If you, as a manager, feel under pressure at work, can you say, honestly, that you do not let it affect you at home? Some of you may think you don't take it home. I wonder whether your partners or children, or even your cat or dog would agree with you! Equally, if you are suffering distress from something which is happening at home, can you ensure that it doesn't affect you at work? We may try our hardest to keep things in their 'proper place', but the nature of stress is such that we are not necessarily aware of the impact it is having on us until something drastic happens.

Stress, whether it originates from events in our personal lives or in the workplace, will, eventually, affect us at work. The longer it is ignored, the greater its impact.

So what is this impact?

Sickness absence

The Health and Safety Executive estimated in 1993 that 30 to 40 per cent of sickness absence is stress-related. The major cause of sickness absence from work is musculo-skeletal problems. Many of these are caused or exacerbated by stress. It is a salutary exercise to work out the cost of sickness absence in your organization, and to find what 40 per cent of that cost is. This amount can be reduced significantly if stress in the workplace is addressed.

Where stress is ignored, the effects worsen and the length of sickness absence increases.

The sickness absence figures of an organization are a good barometer of its own health!

Reduced effectiveness

Many employees are either unaware of, or try to hide, the effect of stress on their health and functioning. This means they are presenting themselves at work and attempting to fulfil their roles; yet it is highly unlikely, given the effects of stress on an individual, that they are functioning at 100 per cent of their capacity. Those who are frightened of being thought incapable by unsympathetic managers or who are fearful of losing their jobs if they take sick leave, will turn up every day for work as though nothing is happening to them, but will produce little to show for it. Not only does this 'presenteeism' cost in lost productivity and effectiveness, but it also has a knock-on effect within the immediate team. If the stressed employee is a manager, the secondary effects are potentially even greater.

Managers can contribute to this presenteeism factor by their attitudes to sickness absence, or their reluctance to take action when they are aware of a distressed employee or the employee's lack of effectiveness or inappropriate behaviour. (This is addressed in Chapter 4.)

Addressing the effects of stress at the earliest possible stage reduces the impact of ineffectiveness. But, while no one would wish to increase the sickness absence in their organization, sometimes employees can cost less and do less damage by taking sick leave whilst the issues are being addressed. A dysfunctional employee cannot be ignored.

Management time

One reason why they cannot be ignored is that management time is an expensive commodity. If an employee is absent from work, a manager has to address the needs of the organization by ensuring that the role of that employee is fulfilled in some way. Schedules, programmes and projects are disrupted. Contingency plans have to be made. And, of course, the employee needs to be supported.

If, however, an employee who is stressed remains at work and is functioning below capacity, often this is not noticed immediately; perhaps not until some major error or disruption has occurred. At this stage, more management time is taken up with picking up the pieces not only of the work itself and of the other staff who are affected but also of the employee who will need much support and attention to become effective again.

As managers know only too well, dealing with others in distress, trying to rectify mistakes, fighting to meet deadlines, taking other staff off important work to make up for lost time, maintaining credibility with customers and clients, all contribute to the pressure on themselves. All increase their stress or their vulnerability to stress.

Stress begets stress. It becomes endemic.

Effect on other employees

Both the absence of employees or their ineffectiveness usually results in more work for their colleagues. More work inevitably means more pressure; it may result in overtime, postponed leave, or the rescheduling of more rewarding work. Too much pressure again will lead to more stress.

Many employees who are experiencing stress at work will find that it affects their relationships with others; they may become less sociable, moody, irritable or aggressive. They may feel others are 'getting at them' or leaving them out. When relationships in a team deteriorate, the effectiveness of the whole team will be reduced. Pressure may then be brought on the whole team to improve, causing resentment, anxiety, or a loss of motivation.

The effects are cumulative and negative. Employees will feel less satisfaction with work and may look for another job as a way of resolving their dissatisfaction.

Retention and recruitment

Employees who are stressed and see no way of resolving a problem in the workplace, may well seek another job. But employees are a valuable resource for the organization. Training and developing employees is costly, but it is an investment in the organization's most expensive resource. It is of benefit both to the employee and the employer. Though some employers may feel that letting stressed employees go is the best solution, it is often a costly error. The employees take with them valuable experience which is difficult to replace. The cost of recruitment and its incumbent training programme far exceeds the cost of supporting one employee through a recovery from stress-related illness.

There is no cheaper way of reducing the impact of stress in the workplace than taking early action.

Accidents and errors

When people are under excessive pressure, they lose their ability to concentrate. In some areas of work, this is likely to lead to increased errors and accidents. The occasional error is human, and may cause a slight hiccup, nothing more. But where precision is paramount, where decisions affect lives, the results may be far-reaching.

Any accident at work is one too many, but an accident by a stressed driver or a machine tool operator, for example, can lead, at best, to expensive claims for compensation and possible prosecution, and, at worse, to death.

Most accidents and errors are avoidable. Where they are the result of an action or lack of action by an employee under stress, the manager may have been able to foresee those results and pre-empt them. The employer may be deemed responsible.

Potential litigation

Litigation in relation to stress at work has crossed the Atlantic and is with us, like it or not. Case law in Britain is beginning to build up, and in the first case in the high courts (Walker v. Northumberland County Council) the social worker concerned was – eventually – awarded £175,000 compensation.

Litigation is big business. But there is much an employer can do to ensure compliance with the laws that govern such issues. (This is the subject of the next chapter.)

Recognizing the existence of stress and taking effective action to reduce or eliminate it in the workplace may well cost far less than any single action in the courts.

Summary

- Stress which is ignored can be expensive.
- Stress contributes to around 40 per cent of sickness absence.
- Early action needs to be taken to avoid the heavy cost of stress.
- Stress begets stress.

Exercises

1. Find out the cost of sickness absence in your organization (or your part of the organization) per year.
2. Work out 40 per cent of this cost.

This is the amount your organization could potentially save by addressing the issue of stress.

CHAPTER 2

The Legal Responsibilities of the Employer

In this chapter we are going to take an overview of the employer's legal responsibilities in relation to employee stress, and look at what recourse to the legal system employees have if they feel that the employer has in some way contributed to their stress-related ill health.

Legislation protecting the health and safety of employees has been in place for many years. However, it has only recently been realized by employers, unions and employees that these laws also encompass protection against the mental ill health of employees. Litigation relating to stress in the workplace has long been big business in America. British companies may well be relieved that we are so far behind; compensation claims relating to stress are only just coming to fruition in Britain. Nevertheless, no organization can afford to be complacent since the effects of stress on an individual may be long term, and claims can be made long after the employee may have left work. Don't, therefore, breathe a sigh of relief when an employee takes ill-health retirement: this could just be the start of some protracted claim that ends up as a court case!

Besides the cost of any compensation awarded to an employee, the employer incurs much expense in investigating claims for compensation even if they are settled out of court. It has been estimated that an average claim could take two years of investigation involving many people (the more senior, and therefore the more expensive, managers) before a decision can be made by insurers. The landmark British case of Walker v. Northumberland County Council (see page 20) took six years from the date of the claim to a decision in the High Court, and another eighteen months awaiting appeal before the council finally settled out of court.

Avoiding legislation by dealing with the underlying causes of stress not only benefits the employee experiencing stress and saves the organization the costs of litigation, but also saves much wasted time and additional pressure for any manager, personnel officer or colleague who is involved in any investigation arising out of a claim. Dealing with stress makes good business sense.

So what is the legislation governing stress in the workplace?

The Health and Safety at Work Etc Act 1974

This act, since its inception, has placed a duty on employers to ensure as far as is reasonably practicable the health and safety of their employees. It is an act which has been taken very seriously by employers who have employed safety officers and adopted stringent policies to safeguard the safety of their employees at work. Physical health has also been addressed by employers who have established occupational health units with screening programmes, advice and guidance on such things as VDU operations and infection control and much more. But what of the mental health aspects?

The Department of Health in their 1993 Health of the Nation campaign drew attention to the mental health aspects of the act, reinforcing the legal responsibilities of employers and offering tentative guidance. Some organizations were addressing 'welfare issues' long before this, and some companies, mostly in the private sector, were offering Employee Assistance Programmes (see Chapter 6). However, until the Walker case with its national publicity, many organizations were unaware of the implications of workplace stress and its detrimental effects on the individual. Now there is no excuse for inaction.

The Management of Health and Safety at Work Regulations 1992

These regulations place a duty on employers to assess the degree to which there is a risk to an employee's health and safety in the workplace, and to take action to reduce and minimize any risk identified. Most employers have complied with the law and conduct risk assessment in relation to physical health and safety. But again, aspects of mental health have, on the whole, been omitted from such assessments.

Conducting risk assessments can be laborious and there is no one correct method. Assigning degrees of risk can be somewhat arbitrary. Chapters 7 and 8 are devoted to taking action and assessing risk to reduce the impact of workplace stress by dealing with common stressors and using a stress inventory.

Enforcing the law

The Health and Safety Executive (HSE) is empowered to prosecute employers who contravene this legislation. Contravention is a criminal offence. In practice, most HSE prosecutions involve breaches of safety and follow from accidents and incidents in the workplace. To date, the HSE has never brought a prosecution under the law against an employer who has failed to take all reasonable steps to ensure the mental health of an employee at work.

However, there is no cause for complacency. Awareness of the legal implications of stress has only recently been heightened. Being the first organization to be prosecuted is not an enviable position for anyone in today's competitive market place!

And it is not only the criminal law which matters. Employees can take action themselves through the civil courts.

The employee's recourse to legal action

Employees who have suffered the ill effects of stress in the workplace can make a claim for compensation for detriment to health and loss of earnings. The employer's insurers will assess the degree to which they believe the organization is culpable, and may or may not make an offer of compensation.

If no offer is made, or if the offer is less than the employee (or their union or legal advisers) deem reasonable, the employee can take the matter further using the civil courts. In doing this, the employee is often supported financially and legally by the union. The onus is on the employee to prove the case. Two relevant laws are the Tort of Negligence and the Law of Contract.

The Tort of Negligence

The Tort of Negligence requires the employee to prove:

- that the employer has a duty of care for the employee (which is implicit in the contract the person has as an employee);
- that there has been a breach of that duty (the 'reasonable man' test is used here); and
- that there was *foreseeable* damage to the person's health.

This last requirement is of vital importance, and I will draw attention to it in later chapters as appropriate. Briefly, if an employer is aware or is made aware that something or someone in the workplace is causing stress to an employee to the degree that their health is impaired, and does nothing to remove or reduce the stressor, then, when the employee's health deteriorates further, the employer would have been expected to *foresee* that the employee's health would deteriorate. Obviously, if there were no indications that health was deteriorating, and no mention of the stressors in the workplace, the employer could not be expected to crystal-gaze.

A superficial look at the Walker case which established the

importance of foreseeability in relation to stress-related illness may be helpful.

Walker v. Northumberland County Council

John Walker was a social work manager who experienced a 'breakdown' in his mental health which he claimed was caused by overwork. He took sick leave, and while he was away from work his manager visited him and discussed his need for support with his workload. Mr Walker was offered additional help on his return to work. This happened. But shortly after his return, the additional help was removed because of pressure elsewhere in the organization, and he was again left to cope with a workload that was too great. He inevitably suffered a deterioration in his mental health, and eventually retired permanently on the grounds of ill health. The High Court judge found against his employers, stating that since they had promised additional help, they were aware of his needs and they could have foreseen that removing that help would have left him vulnerable to the previous pressures. The judge also stated that it was not a defence for the council to claim that lack of resources prevented the continuation of support. The duty of care of an employer is paramount. John Walker accepted £175,000 compensation in an out-of-court settlement just before the case went to appeal.

The Law of Contract

Every employee has a contract of employment which sets out terms and conditions. Some of the terms are 'express', that is, they are stated clearly. Others are implicit in the relationship which exists between employee and employer. To succeed in this civil action, the employee must prove *either* that there has been a breach of an **express term** of the contract *or* a breach of an **implied term.**

An example of the former is a hospital junior doctor who took legal action against his health authority because he was required to work over one hundred hours per week, yet his contract expressly stated his contractual hours were 72. (This case was settled out of court with a payment of £5000.)

An example of an implied term is where an employer is required to take reasonable care of the health and safety of an employee. It is not actually stated in the contract, but implied in the employee–employer relationship. Where reasonable care has not been taken, a breach of the implied term of the contract has occurred.

Industrial tribunals

Lastly, some employees may feel unable to continue with the pressures at work and may retire on the ground of ill health. If they can prove that the employer's action in not dealing with the stress or not providing the necessary support caused or exacerbated their ill health forcing them to leave work, or constitutes negligence or a breach of contract, they can take a case to an industrial tribunal and sue for constructive dismissal.

So as a manager, never be misled into thinking that if you do nothing, and the employees eventually leave, or you suggest they take ill-health retirement, that this is a solution to workplace stress. It could just be the beginning of litigation.

Dealing with compensation claims

If an employee decides to claim damages for stress-related ill health, what happens? How are you, as a manager, involved?

Claims for compensation in these circumstances are no different from claims arising from accidents and injuries at work. The employee has to show that the employer was culpable. Set against this is the individual's responsibility under health and safety regulations for any damage caused to herself. Any compensation will be reduced in proportion to the employee's culpability.

The employer will need to investigate each claim thoroughly to test out its veracity. With a situation of stress, as with some other aspects of ill health, the true extent of the damage may not be realized, or may not occur, until some time after the events – perhaps years later. For this reason, managers must be aware of what evidence they need to keep which might support or refute the employee's case, and should instigate some means for ensuring such records are kept safely and confidentially.

Such evidence will come in many forms:

- notes of informal or formal meetings relating to pressure at work, lack of capability or disciplinary matters (with dates);
- notes of action taken by the manager in support of the employee (with dates and outcomes);
- records of training and development programmes attended and their relationship to known pressures of work (with dates, objectives);
- records of any review meetings drawn up to deal with difficulties (with dates and future action to be taken);
- records of *referral* of an employee to any welfare staff, helping agencies, medical staff, counselling support (*content* of such support should be confidential and therefore not known to a manager);
- details of what support/help is available in confidence either in-house or externally to all employees, with details of publicity and means of access;
- details of any formal policies or procedures used in relation to the employee.

Managers need to be aware that besides providing evidence for internal consideration of a claim, they may be required to appear in court as a witness, even after they have left the organization.

Few employees will take action unless they are sure of their ground because of the additional stress such action will cause over an extended period. And no union or legal adviser will touch cases they believe are groundless.

However, the only way to ensure that your organization avoids litigation is for each manager to take action to prevent stress occurring in the workplace and to support employees who are already experiencing the damaging effects of stress.

Summary

- An employer has a legal responsibility to ensure the physical and mental wellbeing of an employee at work.
- The Health and Safety Executive is empowered to prosecute an employer who contravenes health and safety legislation.
- Employees can take legal action through the civil courts.
- Employees can take their case to an industrial tribunal.

Exercises

1. Familiarize yourself with the requirements of the Health and Safety at Work legislation.
2. Find out what risk assessment strategies have been implemented by your organization.
3. Read Chapter 8 to discover one way of assessing the likelihood of your employees experiencing stress using the workplace stress inventory.

CHAPTER 3
Causes, Symptoms and Effects of Stress

Before we can address the issues of stress in the workplace, we need to develop an understanding of what it is, and how it affects people both personally and in the workplace. It will then become very clear that it is not an issue that should be ignored either for the personal good of an employee or for the good of the organization.

Definitions

There are probably as many definitions of stress as there are people who don't believe it exists! But the one I like best, because of its simplicity and directness, is that of Professor Cary Cooper of The University of Manchester Institute of Science & Technology (UMIST):

Stress is pressure which is too great for us.

Stress is very much a personal issue. Each one of us has our own level of tolerance of pressure at any given time, our own capacity for coping, or not coping with it. We succumb to it at different stages in our lives, we experience it uniquely, and our symptoms can be as varied as our choice of friends.

We can experience pressure from things that are happening in our personal lives in isolation from or in conjunction with the pressures from work. Sometimes we amaze ourselves by the way we seem to cope with juggling twenty-nine balls in the air at one moment, and the next we are floored by what seems, objectively, to be the smallest request from a partner or a boss.

What are your personal stressors?

Write down as many things as you can think of which cause you, or have caused you, stress in your personal life. This can range from the minor stressors, like kids leaving the tops off the toothpaste, to the major, like being burgled.

This is a very useful exercise for each of us to do. It helps us understand ourselves and where our pressures might come from, and it will help you understand where other people's pressures might lie.

In the courses I have presented on this subject, I have been surprised by the variety of responses to this question from managers, some of whom did not admit to ever experiencing any stress in their lives. And yet the biggest surprise was how many stressors we have in common, despite our wide-ranging backgrounds, life experiences, and lifestyles. This list is by no means exhaustive, though it might be exhausting to read!

- any change
- separation
- domestic violence
- sexual abuse
- verbal abuse
- ill health
- ill health of family member
- babies
- divorce
- bereavement
- rape
- harassment
- retirement
- moving house
- disability of self/family
- toddlers

- teenagers
- addictions: drugs, alcohol, cigarettes
- family disputes
- pets
- lack of money
- unemployment
- accidents
- cars
- holidays
- car theft
- assault

- elderly relatives
- schools
- neighbours
- noise
- unexpected expense
- disasters: minor/major
- injuries
- travel
- burglary
- road rage
- house repairs
- balancing home and work

Most of us have experienced one or more of these in our lifetime, and have probably been able to cope, with or without the personal support of family, friends or professional counsellors. But if we experience a number of them together or within a short time scale and/or we don't have the support or professional help we need, they may be too much for us to cope with. It is then that our bodies begin to tell us that the pressures are too great.

Before we look at how we cope, or what happens when we don't cope, let's look at some of the pressures we face at work.

What are your stressors at work?

Write down as many things as you can think of which are causing you or have caused you to feel pressurized at work. These can range from the minor irritants, like losing a piece of paper, to the major, like having an argument with the boss.

Again, this is another useful exercise, and one which you might wish to do with your own team members at a later stage. The responses I have received on courses have two common roots or themes which seemed to run through many, if not all, suggestions, and which are a good indicator of where, as a manager, you can help put things right. See if you can identify them as you read the list.

- buildings
- facilities
- hours of work
- unsocial hours
- overtime – planned and unplanned
- changes in the work environment
- telephones ringing
- managers!
- harassment
- racism
- unreasonable behaviour
- people who don't deliver
- lack of interest
- lack of trust
- being isolated
- personality conflicts
- job not clear
- conflicting roles
- unclear lines of reporting
- too many responsibilities
- boring work
- no involvement in decision making
- too many decisions to make
- not enough participation
- organizational attitudes to absence, discipline, capability
- lack of development opportunities
- lack of promotion opportunities
- unreasonable bars to promotion
- lack of interest of manager
- lack of support from manager

- work stations
- lighting
- levels/quantity of work
- shift work
- technology

- travelling problems

- furniture
- subordinates!
- bullying
- sexism
- employee complaints
- or don't deliver on time
- lack of commitment
- lack of respect
- being overcrowded
- unfriendliness
- too many bosses
- conflict in role
- not enough work
- too much work
- work too repetitive
- too many rules

- lack of communication
- lack of consultation

- unfair access to training

- appraisals
- fear of redundancy
- fear of redeployment
- threat of others being better than self

This list has come from a number of managers; it would probably not be much longer or different if we compiled it from the views of a cross-section of workers in an organization. Managers, after all, are also employees; they, too, have expectations, fears and needs. Nevertheless, the list tells us much about what could be wrong at work, and the point is, if managers, who have more power and control over their working lives than others, feel like this, what is it like being on the shop floor, or at the bottom of a hierarchy?

> If you haven't yet worked out any common themes or roots, read the list again and make a mark against all those which are about people or lack of control or both. Have you got many unmarked items?

People, wherever they are in an organization, are a source of much stress for others. Even as a manager, you cannot be in total control of what others do, what they say, how they behave, how they react. We are all individual, all unique. And all of us have a limited span of control over our lives. *This is the greatest stressor for most of us: not being in control.*

Managing our own stress is about taking control of ourselves and our lives. (See Chapter 10.)

Managing employee stress in the workplace, as a manager, is more about understanding other people's stressors and taking action to reduce them within the framework of the organization's goals. The effectiveness of the two-way communication process between the manager and the employee is therefore crucial in identifying potential stressors and their resolution.

And this is very important in trying to understand stress. You as a person, as a manager, can't possibly know what it's like for your employees. You can't know what is right for them. For example, if you look again at the list, you will see that it is full of contradictions: too much work, too little work, too isolated, too crowded. Your role is to *find out*, at an individual level, what the stressors are, and you can only do this by talking to, and listening to, your staff.

If you read the list again, with the theme of communication in mind, you can see where talking to employees, improving methods of communication even within your sphere of control, if not throughout the whole organization, could resolve some issues immediately.

We share some stressors; others are unique to us. Those we share can be dealt with at the organizational level, those which are unique to us can be dealt with at an individual level. It is not as complicated as might seem at first and is dealt with in further detail in the following chapters.

Symptoms and effects of stress

So what happens when we experience too many pressures to cope with? Stress affects both our physical body and our mental processes; in turn, these both affect how we behave under extreme pressure, and the degree to which we can continue to perform our roles, at home and at work, efficiently and effectively

When we face any challenge, whether it's a physical threat, verbal abuse or mental cruelty, we are programmed biologically to either fight it or run away from it (the so-called fight or flight syndrome). Our bodies go into 'red alert' mode: our autonomic nervous system has been triggered by messages from the brain. Hormones (adrenalin, noradrenalin and cortisol) are released into our bloodstream. Our pupils dilate; our hearing becomes more acute; our digestive system closes down and our mouths go dry; our immune system shuts down; we sweat more; our muscles tense; our heart rate increases and our blood pressure rises.

In this way, our bodies are prepared for an immediate *physical* reaction to a perceived threat. But this happens not just when we are facing physical danger, but when we are facing an irate boss or customer, a difficult situation, an interview, a traffic jam. Our bodies are geared up for fight or flight, but we cannot do either. We cannot run away from a difficult work situation, however much we might like to; we cannot fight an irate customer because we would almost certainly lose our jobs. But if these stressors, these triggers for our physical survival mechanisms, aren't removed, we remain in the physical state of preparedness. And this can be dangerous. It was only ever intended as a temporary state.

If, therefore, this physical state continues without release or relief for any length of time, we face long-term negative effects. Our bodies are unable to tolerate the condition we are in. Their natural response to stress, designed to enable us to cope, can therefore lead to ill health and even to death. The problem is, our bodies were never programmed to cope with the stresses of post-industrial life which by their very nature do not require physical exertion.

If nothing is done to remove or reduce the causes of the stress, and we continue to react in the way described above, our physical and mental health will deteriorate.

So what are the effects of our reaction to stress?

Physical effects

The physical effects range from the minor, perhaps leading to a few days' sickness or discomfort, to the severe, leading to months of absence and maybe to ill-health retirement. Whether minor or major, one day's absence or ill-health retirement, there is a cost to the employer which, as we have seen, does not rest with the one employee. Physical symptoms can include:

- headaches
- neck aches
- tightness across the chest
- palpitations
- heartburn
- exhaustion
- constipation
- loss of appetite
- nausea
- backaches
- breathlessness
- sweating
- indigestion
- tiredness
- sleeplessness
- diarrhoea
- increased appetite
- migraine

- nervous twitching
- stuttering

- trembling
- upset stomach

The list is almost endless.

Mental effects

The mental effects can have a greater impact on the workplace since they do not necessarily indicate to those experiencing them that they need help. Employees may be unaware of, or unable to face up to, their changed state of wellbeing and often insist that they are fine. Yet they can do untold damage to inter-personal relations, to effectiveness and efficiency.

The symptoms below are not ones that would cause any of us necessarily to take time off from work. Indeed, for many of us, they are what we accept as part of 'modern day' living. Look at the list below from the point of view of a being a manager responsible for the output of the team and you will understand the knock-on effects of people in this frame of mind. The list, again, is not exhaustive:

- irritability
- difficulty in decision making
- loss of sense of humour
- difficulty in concentrating
- depression
- uncooperative behaviour
- fear of being alone
- lack of care over appearance
- feeling of being unable to cope
- passive

- aggressiveness
- feeling of failure
- withdrawal
- anxiety
- over-activity
- dread
- lack of interest in life
- loss of libido
- paranoia
- tearful

The above lists are presented to give you an idea of the range of effects stress can have on an individual. Not all of the above symptoms by themselves indicate that stress is being experienced. In fact, some of the physical symptoms may well be indications of other underlying medical problems. Stress may or may not play a part in these. However, people experiencing stress are more susceptible to minor illnesses and ailments, and who can say whether the backache experienced by so many of us comes from heavy lifting, working at a VDU or indeed from tensing our muscles under stress?

No manager is expected to be a medical expert who can diagnose health problems, nor to be an 'agony aunt' offering advice and wisdom. The manager's role in dealing with stress in the workplace is more straightforward, as we shall see.

Summary

- We experience stress when we are no longer able to cope with all the pressures on us at a specific time.
- Stress is personal to us, though we may have many stressors in common with others.
- Stress often stems from not being or feeling in control and from other people.
- Stress results in both physical and mental ill health.
- If stressors are not dealt with, our health can deteriorate.
- Communication is a key to managing stress.

Exercises

If you haven't already done so while you were reading this chapter,

1. Make a list of all those things which cause you stress in your personal life.
2. Make a list of all those things in the workplace which cause you stress.
3. Identify those which are caused by other people or by you not being in control of a situation.
4. Identify those which you feel might be improved by better communication.
5. Think about where you could improve communication with your team.

These exercises will give you some understanding of what your employees might be experiencing. While you are reading the book, remember you are also an employee and can seek support and action about your stressors from your own manager.

CHAPTER 4
The Role of the Manager

The manager in any organization has a crucial and pivotal role in dealing with stress in the workplace and with employees experiencing stress. However, the organization itself has a large responsibility for ensuring that mechanisms are in place both to support employees and to support a manager in taking action to address the issues of stress in the workplace. In addition, the organization, through its insurers, protects the individual manager against personal claims of negligence or lack of care.

The importance of people management

As a manager, you are in the best position of anyone in the organization to look after the health and safety needs of the employee on a day to day basis; those managers who take a cavalier attitude to stress and its effects do so at the risk of leaving their employers open not just to litigation, but to being less productive and efficient, and thus less competitive in the market place.

It has long been a joke among managers that their job would be so much easier if they didn't have any people to manage! Though we may be amused by such throwaway remarks, it is true that many managers feel much more comfortable with systems, programmes and machinery rather than with people. Indeed, many managers reach their level precisely because they have been excellent at the operational end of the business, not because they are 'people persons'.

However, people management is not an optional extra for any manager. Without the people, there would be no goods, no services, no contacts with customers, no profits. People are an organization's most valuable resource, its most expensive asset. And ignoring employees and their needs is the most costly mistake a manager can make. The manager's role is to manage the employees who make up the team in order to achieve the objectives of the team, the unit, the department, the organization as a whole. A dysfunctional team member affects the working of the whole team, its collective spirit, its interpersonal relationships, its output, its contribution to the efficiency of the organization.

So what can you, as an overworked manager, do to ensure the wellbeing of all the members of your team? Essentially, you need an understanding of what stress is, how it is caused, how it can be recognized, how you can support those experiencing it and how it can be addressed in the workplace. But firstly, however, you need to start with yourself.

The manager's self-awareness

As a manager, you need to ensure that you know how to look after yourself. Being aware of your own feelings, discomforts, excessive pressures, and your own state of stress will pay dividends when it comes to understanding and helping others. Remember, you are as vulnerable as the next employee, manager or director to excess pressure and its detrimental effects. By recognizing and acknowledging your own state of wellbeing and by taking action to put things right for yourself, you will be in a positive position to be aware of the state of wellbeing of your staff, and you will be more effective as a manager. *Managers who are experiencing excessive pressures themselves often create a stressful environment for others.*

Look again at the list of symptoms on page 31. How many

of these are you experiencing now, or have you experienced in the past few months? How contented do you feel with life in general, and how happy are you with the situation at work? Do you dread the thought of work? Are you just going through the motions? Or are you still enthusiastic and excited by your role?

The science of stress is still in its infancy, and will probably always be inexact. Measures to assess one's vulnerability to stress have been devised, and are interesting exercises to undertake. But most people, if only they could stop themselves for one minute to think about how they are feeling, could give a pretty accurate description of their state of wellbeing. And if you can't do this for yourself, listen to your partner, your children, your parents, your work colleagues. Have they recently told you how irritable, withdrawn, miserable, or tetchy you are being? An irritable or inconsistent manager, for example, will not get the best from the staff: they may feel threatened, anxious, unclear of what is expected of them, fearful of what will be said or done next. And we all know the knock-on effects of our moods on those we live with.

Having assessed your current state of health, what can you do about the stress you are already experiencing, or what can you do to protect yourself from the ill effects? Chapter 10 looks in some detail at how we can help ourselves. You may, of course, feel that you need to talk to your own manager about some of the issues for you.

The stigma of stress

Recognizing the signs of stress in others is no mean feat. People who feel vulnerable at work will often go to extraordinary lengths to hide what is happening to them. The stigma of stress still exists. People are fearful of being thought incompetent, emotional or unfit for the job. They are afraid of being side-stepped, demoted or even losing their job.

Being stressed is not a function of an individual *per se*, but a function of all the pressures on that individual and their ability to cope at a given point in time. Remove or reduce the stressors, support the individual, and the symptoms and effects diminish and disappear. Most people experiencing stress can and do make a full recovery. Admitting to feeling stressed should not condemn someone for life. Rather, it is a sign of their strength and self-awareness that they are aware of difficulties and wish to deal with them.

If, as a manager, you give the impression that you think stress is a weakness, and that employees who experience its ill effects should be dismissed, you are closing an opportunity for communication which allows you to recognize and deal with workplace stress. You are ensuring that the effects will accumulate until little can be done. You are exacerbating the individual's problems, and potentially that of other employees and costing your organization a lot of money.

Sometimes, it is the organizational culture which perpetuates the myths about stress. This is widespread and damaging, but can still be overcome by individual managers who are concerned for their staff.

Recognizing the signs of stress in others

There is no simple answer to the question about how any manager can know who is experiencing stress. You can look at the list of symptoms and wonder who might be experiencing them. But who is going to tell you? And could they not be symptoms of other illnesses? But there are clues which indicate very clearly that things are not right for someone.

People's behaviour in the workplace is often the best indicator of the existence of too much pressure for them. What you need to be alert to is *any change from a person's normal behaviour at work.* If a previously diligent employee suddenly becomes slap-happy and careless, if a previously gregarious person retreats into corners, goes for lone walks, or leaves work early to avoid the drink in the pub, if a normally well-dressed colleague suddenly shows no interest in the state of his clothes, then something is wrong.

Knowing your staff

To know when someone's behaviour has changed, you need to know how they normally behave, and that means knowing your staff well. If you are a senior manager, this does not mean knowing all the members of each team, but you will need to know the team leaders, and it will be *their* responsibility to know their own team members. In this way, no unreasonable assumptions are being made in the plea to know your staff well.

If one of your middle managers is exhibiting signs of being stressed, the likelihood is that he is affecting all the staff in that team. If you are able to support that manager, this will have a positive benefit for the whole team.

In some circumstances (and all too frequently) an employee can be experiencing stress for some time, maybe weeks or months, with no recognition by the manager. Your attention may be drawn to this employee because of a *disciplinary matter* or a matter of *lack of capability*. It is a sign that an organization is not concerned about the wellbeing of its employees, and does not have the right mechanisms for dealing with distressed staff, if the first indication that something is wrong is a disciplinary interview. The likelihood is that that person's work or behaviour did not deteriorate overnight. A good manager will pick up the signs long before such drastic measures need to be taken.

Another clue is the *sickness absence* record of a member of staff or group of staff. Patterns of absence may develop which should alert a manager. The regular day off over a long period of time may indicate an inability to cope with the pressures of a given situation. A long period of absence with medical certificates stating stress, anxiety, depression, stomach upsets, should again ring warning bells. Something is not right, and the likelihood is that there were signs *before* the employee took sick leave.

Lastly, a further indication of distress may manifest itself when you least expect it, for example when you are meeting with a member of your staff on a one-to-one basis behind closed doors. Perhaps you are conducting a staff appraisal, or you are jointly reviewing the progress of a project. You may innocently ask a simple question, or be drawing attention to a minor error, and suddenly you are on the receiving end of an *uncharacteristic verbal attack*, or the person dissolves into *tears*. (Both these situations may arise equally with male or female members of staff.) These emotional responses may be the clearest sign you have that they have been bottling something up, and that you have unearthed a little part of it.

Remember, in each of the situations outlined above, the root cause of the behaviour, the outburst, the absence, the shoddy work, may not be pressure from work, but from their personal lives. However, if the employee is affected at work, it needs to be of concern to you as a manager whatever the source of the stress.

So how can you approach any of these situations without intruding, without exacerbating matters, without becoming unduly pressurized yourself and reacting accordingly?

Approaching the problem

You are now aware of, or have been made aware of, a problem with an individual's behaviour, quality of work or demeanour. It is a delicate situation, and you need to think about some fundamental issues before you step in with your well-intentioned advice or your size-ten boots! Just because you are a manager, employees are not going to open up and tell you all. Certain conditions may be necessary:

- the need for privacy;
- the need for absolute confidentiality;
- the need to feel unthreatened;
- the need for your undivided attention;
- the right not to tell you about their private lives.

You will also need to consider, without feeling personally affronted, that you might not be the right person for them to talk to because:

- you are the wrong gender (think of sexual abuse or marital problems);

- you are the key to their future promotion;
- you disciplined them last year and that's your perceived role;
- a colleague whom you admire is the cause of their problems;
- you are the problem;
- you remind them of someone of whom they are afraid;

There will be other reasons. Remember though, unless you are the problem, their reluctance to talk to you is not about you as a person but who or what you represent. Take it professionally, not personally. But make sure you give them the option to talk to someone else, in confidence, if they are uncomfortable with you. Where issues need to be dealt with, you will be involved. Offering another listener is not abdicating your responsibility, nor is it being undermined. It is the action of a good manager.

Broaching the subject

You have noticed a problem. You now have a responsibility to do something about it (remember *foreseeability*). You therefore need to set up an initial meeting with the person concerned, without making them feel that they are going to be 'carpeted'. If you already operate an open door policy, this won't be a problem. If you don't, how you broach the subject is paramount. Compare the two approaches:

> 'James, I'd like to see you in my room at
> two o'clock today.'

and

> 'James, I'd just like to have a quick word with you.
> Would two o'clock in my room suit you?'

The first would probably feel threatening and authoritarian to most people, and if they are under stress they are likely to feel this even more acutely. The second is more friendly and encouraging, and is more likely to aid further communication.

Preparing for the meeting

There is much at stake in this initial meeting. For it to be productive how, where and in what circumstances it takes place are all-important. The more open and friendly the meeting and the fewer the barriers, physical or otherwise, between you and the employee, the more likely you are to uncover any problem and be able to start to address the issues. You may, therefore, wish to consider the following:

- Is the meeting room private (eg not overlooked by the work area, other people)?
- Is the seating comfortable?
- Have you ensured that you will not be disturbed?
- Have you left plenty of time before your next meeting? (If the employee opens up, the last thing you need to do is to stop them.)
- If you're going to have tea or coffee, have it ready.
- You may need a box of tissues – be prepared.

These may sound somewhat trivial, but they often make the difference between success and failure in achieving the purpose.

So what is the purpose of this meeting?

Purpose of the meeting

As the saying goes, if you don't know where you're going, how do you know when you've got there? You therefore need to be clear *before the meeting* what you hope to achieve. Consider the following purposes:

- to let an employee know that you are aware of something not being right and that you are willing to help them;
- to give an employee an opportunity to talk to you or to someone else about issues which might be distressing them;
- to explore whether there are any workplace issues involved;
- to work with the employee to find options or solutions;
- to offer support personally or from a professional body;
- to set up a process to monitor and review the situation.

There will be many possible outcomes of such a meeting depending on the emotional state of the person, the interaction between you, how much they want to or can reveal of the problem, the personal nature of the problem, whether confidentiality is an issue which prevents further action being taken, whether they prefer to talk to someone else, or wish to be referred to an outside agency. And so on.

Essentially, therefore, you need to approach the meeting with an open mind and a willingness to be flexible. Anything can happen, anything can be revealed.

Summary

- Managers are in the best position to deal with stress in the workplace.
- Managers need to be aware of their own vulnerabilities to stress.
- There is still a stigma attached to stress which means employees are afraid to admit it.
- A manager needs to be aware of clues which indicate a stressed employee:
  - a change in their behaviour
  - a disciplinary matter
  - lack of capability
  - sickness absence
  - outburst – anger, tears.
- Before addressing the issues, managers need to consider whether they are the right people to deal with the issues.
- How the manager approaches the employee is crucial.
- The meeting venue needs to be prepared in advance.
- The manager should be clear about the purpose of the meeting.

Exercises

1. Ensure that you know the staff who work for you directly. If you feel you don't, make a point of spending time with them to get to know them better.

2. Take time each day to think about yourself and how you are feeling.
3. Be alert to the behaviour of your staff, and take immediate action if you notice any uncharacteristic behaviour.
4. Check sickness absence records of your staff regularly and follow up any noticeable patterns which suggest that something other than ill health may be causing problems.

CHAPTER 5
Communicating Effectively

Communication is the key to managing stress, and yet many of us have had no training in developing effective communication skills. Such training can be beneficial not only when dealing with employees experiencing stress but in every facet of our personal and business lives.

Developing communication and listening skills

Effective communication saves precious time. It can help you get to the heart of an issue quickly and in a supportive manner; it will encourage an employee to be more open with you; and it will enable you to take effective action at an early stage.

Let's start with the first meeting you have with an employee who you believe is experiencing stress or whose performance or behaviour is causing you concern. The aim of the meeting will be to uncover any underlying issues which may be causing or contributing to the employee's dysfunction or distress, and to explore possible options and solutions. Some of the issues might not be clear even to the person experiencing them. Their state of stress may have reduced their ability to think clearly or logically about what has been happening, why, and how it has left them feeling. They need help in sorting this out for themselves. At some stage they may also need professional help (see Chapter 6). But to begin with, they are talking to you, as their manager.

What, then, is required of you?

Building rapport

There are three interacting elements in the process of any communication: yourself, the other person, and the environment in which the communication takes place.

Both you and the other person will bring 'baggage' from previous experiences to the meeting, from your views of the world and from your views of each other. This baggage may get in the way of the communication process, and it will be your role as the manager to remove any of the barriers between you to facilitate the process of communication. These barriers take many forms: language, culture, personality, behaviour, emotional state, dress, role, expectations of each other, relative power.

Equally, there will be physical barriers related to the room in which you meet, for example the way the furniture is set out, the privacy and confidentiality afforded by the location, the ambience of the room.

You will need to think about these issues before the meeting, and to address any which are within your power to do something about. Your aim is for *congruence* between the three elements. Set the scene before the meeting to ensure that the environment is non-threatening, supportive, friendly, quiet, and confidential. Make sure you will not be disturbed by others or by the telephone. Make sure you don't sit with a desk between you (think of modern doctor's surgeries). Even plants and pictures signify something reassuring.

When you meet with employees, you need to build rapport with them so they trust you and feel confident that you are there to help them. Aim to see and understand things from the employees' point of view, not from your own. Be yourself, not the person you would like to be or the person you think the employees want you to be. Respect the differences between you, whether they are differences of style, language, experiences, educational background or any others.

Building rapport is not about having inconsequential conversations about the weather or someone's family before getting down to business. It is about making the other person feel comfortable with you, being genuine, warm and empathetic and showing them respect as a person.

The following strategies will help establish and maintain rapport:

● Allow employees to sit themselves comfortably, and at the right distance from you for their comfort (we all need different amounts of personal space).
● Remember, a desk puts a barrier between you that words will not be able to overcome.
● Maintain eye contact without staring. Holding eye contact shows that you are listening, that they have your attention, and that you are interested in what they are saying.
● Don't fidget (put away paper clips, pens and other distractions before you start if you have a tendency to fidget − it can be very distracting for the other person).
● Don't make notes while you are listening. If you are actively listening (see below) you will find you remember all the salient points for any notes you need to make later.
● Don't allow yourself to be distracted by telephones, movements outside, loud noises, laughter. The exception is the fire alarm!
● Try to look relaxed and welcoming. Facial expressions reveal much, and body posture says everything: avoid folding your arms, avoid sitting sideways, avoiding hunching yourself (however threatened you may be feeling). Make yourself comfortable, and you will look at ease. Take your cues from how the other person is sitting.

Active listening

Anyone with responsibility for people needs to develop good listening skills. To be a good listener is more, much more, than passively listening to someone. And the best way to learn is to practise. On paper, listening skills may well seem false and theoretical. However, good listening skills are vital in any interaction between people and are intended to enhance the communication process. They can be used in everyday interactions, not just in your role as a manager, but as a parent, a partner, a colleague, a friend or a relative.

If you are dealing with a distressed employee – one who may be retreating into his shell, or is tearful or responding aggressively – you will need to use different techniques to facilitate the interaction.

Active listening is also more than just giving employees space to tell their story. It is about encouraging them appropriately. It is about balancing the need to say enough to show you are listening and clarifying what you don't understand, and taking over the session. While silences are important, so is the nodding of the head, the occasional 'uh-huh' or 'hmm' which indicate you are attending. In addition, there are a number of ways in which you can interact with employees which are designed to encourage them to open up, to continue, to explore their thoughts and feelings (see below).

These techniques should be used appropriately when the speakers seem stuck, confused, have lost the thread of what they were saying, or perhaps when they have recovered from a tearful moment.

They should never be used to interrupt employees mid-flow. Not only is this disrespectful, but it will interrupt their train of thought and make them feel devalued; it may feel to them as if you haven't been listening or that you want to take over. If you are confused by what you have heard (a distressed person will not necessarily tell a story in a logical sequence) then a natural pause may allow you to seek clarification of an issue.

Using silences
There are times when people need a silence and have stopped talking for this purpose. They may wish to have time to recover if they have become emotional, to reformulate their thoughts if they are confused, to reflect on what they have

already told you, to think about options. If you jump in too quickly, you may inhibit them and their thought processes. Only if they seem uncomfortable with the length of silence should you break it. Use one of the techniques below when you do so.

To begin with, you may feel uncomfortable with silences. Most of us do. It's worth practising this skill, if only to avoid conveying your discomfort to the other person, thus adding to their pressures.

Using open questions

Closed questions are ones which usually require a one-word answer and give you very little information. They do nothing to move a person forward, although in certain circumstances they might answer an important question or give vital information. For example,

- 'On which day did this happen?'

Open questions, on the other hand, encourage the speaker to open up, and allow him to clarify, to expand, to explore the feelings involved, to tell you more. For example,

- 'How did you feel when ...'
- 'What else happened to make you feel threatened?'
- 'What happened after ...'

You need to be aware before you ask a question what its purpose is, and the best way of achieving that purpose. An inadvertently closed question can always be followed up with an open one to encourage further response. As with everything in life, practice improves performance.

Reflecting

Reflecting is 'giving back' the speaker's words and feelings to encourage her to elaborate or to continue if he has 'dried up'. It allows you to let her know you are listening, and enables you to check that you have fully understood what she is saying or feeling. If you've got it wrong, it gives her the opportunity to correct you:

- *'You felt humiliated by Mary ...'*
- *'So, while you were struggling to write the report, he ...'*

Paraphrasing

After you have listened to a story for a short while, you may need to check that you have understood what you have been told and its significance for the speaker. By paraphrasing his words you again convey that you have been actively listening, thus reinforcing his feelings of being valued. It also gives him the chance to clarify any confusions, to explain anything you might have misunderstood or misinterpreted. Don't underestimate the value of this. If as a manager you have to take any action about what you have heard, you will need to be absolutely clear about the situation, otherwise you may find yourself unwittingly exacerbating the existing distress of the employee.

Paraphrasing also serves the purpose of allowing the employee to hear his story as if it is someone else's. Confusions, inconsistencies, significance, and perspective may all be altered by this. While it may be uncomfortable for the speaker to hear the story again, it will help clarify his view of what has been happening:

- *'Let me make sure I understand this fully. You were upset a few weeks ago when I asked you to let Jane help you with the project. You felt I was undermining you. And now you feel that Jane thinks you're incompetent and is withholding further work from you. You also said ...'*

Focusing

This is a very useful technique when you are trying to sift out the most important, the most salient parts of a story. It encourages the speaker to give more information about an issue, to explore particular areas which she might have difficulty with, to focus her attention on the significant aspects, or indeed to put you right if you're homing in on insignificant events!

The technique involves focusing on a particular event,

maybe a word or a phrase which seems important, and to play it back to the speaker:

- *'You mentioned the noise levels in room five. Can you tell me a bit more about this?'*
- *'You said earlier that Fred dumped things on you. Can you tell me what you meant by that?'*

Exploring options

You are not expected to resolve other people's problems for them, nor to decide for them what they should do. The onus lies with the individual concerned. There are very good reasons for this. First, you may not have all the facts of the situation (employees may withhold certain information for whatever reason); second, you cannot experience what the employees themselves are experiencing, so any advice or suggestions you might make may not be the right ones for them; third, unless the employee is committed to a solution, it will not be successful; this means any solution 'imposed' on an employee is doomed to failure.

So what is your role in this respect? Frequently the people experiencing the problem are aware of possible courses of action to resolve issues. Their problem is in exploring these and their potential outcomes. Using the techniques outlined above, you can help employees think about the options to decide what might be best for them. If they are devoid of ideas, perhaps because they are too close to the situation, you can offer possibilities. The essence of this is that as a manager, you can only *offer* not *impose* options or solutions.

The bonus for you is that if the options chosen are unsuccessful, you should not be blamed!

It is often tempting to offer advice particularly when the employee is distressed: 'If I were you, I would ...' But you are not them. So never offer advice which they feel they have to take. This can add to their burden. It might add to yours if it turns out to be wrong advice!

Summarizing

At the end of your initial exploratory meeting (and any meeting with them, in fact), it is useful to summarize all the main points as you understand them, and if you have explored options for resolving issues or taking the matters further, to reiterate the options and any further actions either of you have agreed to take. This will clarify for both of you what the issues are and what is going to happen next. Allow the employee to correct any misunderstandings, and to seek any clarification on their role or action or your promises of action. This summary will provide you with the essence of your notes for any records you need to keep (see Chapter 2).

Summarizing is a useful way to end a session, bringing it to a tidy close so all the loose ends are gathered up and all parties are aware of what will happen next.

Arrange your next meeting with the employee, and after he has gone, document the meeting, while ensuring that you protect confidentiality.

The exploratory meeting in practice

Let us now return to the initial exploratory meeting you have set up with the employee you are concerned about. You have decided your purpose, you have prepared the environment, and you have approached the employee. What happens next?

The most crucial part of any meeting is the beginning. It sets the scene for what follows. I have therefore provided scenarios for the different circumstances and the reactions you might get. Obviously, we all have our own ways of dealing with interactions, so there is nothing prescriptive in what is here. It is for you to take or leave as you wish. If you feel totally confident about the opening session, if you know your staff well, if you have done this successfully numerous times before, then skip the section.

Scenario 1: If you've noticed a change in someone's behaviour

In this scenario, you have little more than a hunch that

something might not be right, and your purpose is to give the employee an opportunity to talk to you, and for you to offer them appropriate help or support. You are not intending to intrude, and you recognize that if there are issues, and particularly if these are personal, it is the employee's right not to disclose anything.

- *'I've noticed that you don't seem your usual self. I wonder if you'd like to talk to me, or to someone else, in confidence, about how you are feeling?'*

This is an offer to the employee; it is non-threatening, impartial, and guarantees confidentiality to them. Her reaction may be:

Denial

- *'I'm fine. I don't need to talk to anyone.'*

Your response:

- *'Well, if you ever feel you need to talk to anyone, whether it's about work or personal issues, just ask me, or you could arrange to see Sarita, the welfare officer.'*

You have opened avenues of communication. You have given options. You have not intruded. The chances are that if employees feel you are genuine, they'll come back. You should still monitor their work or behaviour, and if it continues to cause concern, then move to Scenario 2.

Acceptance

- *'Everything's gone wrong. I don't know where to begin.'*

This is the most helpful response for you. The employee wishes to talk about the issues, but needs a helping hand in starting off and perhaps in continuing. The listening skills above should enable you to handle this meeting effectively.

Aggression

- *'What the hell's it got to do with you? It's private!'*

Here is an admittance that things are wrong, but a lack of acceptance that you or anyone else can do anything to help, or a fear of vulnerability.

Your response:

- *'I just want you to know I'm here if you want to talk about anything. If you don't that's fine. But if you find that it's interfering with your work, let me know and we can talk about ways we might be able to support you.'*

Again, it's an unconditional offer, not intrusive, not threatening. But also, it's a subtle reminder that if something is affecting work, you want to know. If your organization has a welfare or a counselling service, you could let the employee have an access number for future use.

It is counter-productive to retaliate, get angry or take such a reaction personally. It may be the wrong time for them to disclose what is happening: they may not feel safe enough. But they now know that you've noticed, and that you have offered support. And if things deteriorate, the following scenario may be appropriate.

Scenario 2: If sickness records, behaviour or incompetence are in question
Here you can be more direct in your opening:

- *'I'm aware that your work is not up to its usual standard/you've had several periods of sickness last month/you are having difficulty working with John. I'd like to have a chat with you about the situation at work at the moment.'*

Where this meets with denial or aggression, you can be more specific about what you as a manager expect in a work situation:

- *'I understand that you don't want to talk about personal issues, but as you know, this is a very busy section, and other people rely on us to achieve our deadlines. That means all of us working together. Your behaviour/absence/work is causing me some concern, and I'd like to see if there's anything I can do to help you.'*

A further negative response at this stage requires clarity of what action you will take if the situation does not improve:

- *'I understand your position. My position is that I'll review the situation in two weeks, and if there hasn't been an improvement, and you still don't wish to talk to me or anyone else about the issues that might be contributing to this, then I will have no alternative but to use the formal policies of the company. I can let you have a copy of these, if you would like. But remember, I'm here to help you. You're one of my team. All you have to do is ask.'*

This is clear, it's professional and it still leaves the way open. It might be perceived as threatening, but you have a responsibility to your organization for the efficiency of your part of the service. You are being fair.

Some employees in this situation may be receiving help from a counselling service either through the workplace or privately. This will be confidential, and it is every person's right to maintain that confidentiality, even if you feel it might not be in their best interest to do so. You do *not* need to know about it. If they are seeking help, it is likely that you will notice an improvement. If there is no improvement, you will be taking the next step, anyway.

These two scenarios provide suggestions of how you might handle an employee's response to your setting up an exploratory meeting with him. They are offered as ways of defusing potentially explosive situations and of making clear what your role is both in relation to offering support to the employee but also in fulfilling your operational functions to the organization.

After the meeting

A record needs to be kept of every contact you have with an employee whose behaviour is causing you some concern or who is experiencing some stress, even if he has refused to disclose anything to you. There are three reasons for this:

- to be able to measure progress;
- to have an accurate record of the interaction, whatever its outcome;
- to protect you and/or the organization in the event of any future complaint or claim for compensation.

Agreeing the record

Agreeing the content of your notes of the meeting with the employee concerned has more than one purpose. First, it ensures that you share perspectives. Where you don't and these differences cannot be resolved by further discussion, a record should be made of the differing perspectives. Second, it shows respect for the employee which will build on your relationship with her. Lastly, should any dispute arise in the future an agreed record can act as an arbiter.

Confidentiality

If you have been told something in confidence, you should respect this. The trust an employee has in you depends on this. You might wish to decide at the beginning of a meeting which issues can remain confidential and in this case you must let the employee know *before* he discloses anything to you. For example, you could make it clear that a disciplinary offence would be noted and action taken.

However, personal stories have no place in an employee record unless the employee wishes them to be noted for a particular purpose. An example of this might be marital breakdown. If the employee wishes this to be used in mitigation or believes it has a bearing on other issues, then this can be noted. Check, however, that the employee is aware of the implications of it being kept in writing.

Equally, an employee may have disclosed that he has been experiencing harassment, but does not wish to take formal action at present. (You can still take action in the case of harassment in an indirect way – see Case Study 3, pages 96–100.) Yet he may want you to keep a record in case he wishes to take action at a future stage.

Remember that you can keep an accurate record without breaking confidentiality if you are careful about the wording; for example, 'Jane feels she is being harassed by another member of the team. I agreed to take no direct action at present because she is afraid, but have agreed to monitor the situation and discuss it with her in two weeks' time.'

Summary

- The initial exploratory meeting with the employee is the most important one.
- During the meeting, a range of listening skills can be used to help the flow, to encourage the employee and to explore the issues.
- The success of the initial meeting depends on how the opening is handled.
- Avoid taking employee reactions personally.
- There are a number of ways of opening channels of communication to the reluctant or aggressive employee which balance the needs of the employee and the organization.
- Acceptance, denial and aggression are the most common responses to first approaches and need to be handled sensitively.

Exercises

1. Practise using the suggestions given about your body language and preparation for the meeting when dealing with non-sensitive issues. Reflect on any differences you notice in the communication process.
2. Practise different listening skills in everyday communication, allowing others the real opportunity to tell you about things which are important to them without interrupting them or waiting to say your bit. Is the outcome any different from normal?

3. In any conflict you experience, whether at home or at work, use the strategies in the two scenarios given to defuse the situation. Make a note of what strategies seem to work for you, or for different people.
4. Set up a recording system for dealing with people experiencing stress, preferably in consultation with other managers. Such a system should include a note on:

- what support has been offered;
- what action is being taken, where appropriate, to reduce or remove the stressors;
- what form of monitoring will take place.

CHAPTER 6
Supporting the Employee at Work

Addressing the issue of stress in the workplace is two-pronged. First, provide support for employees who are already experiencing stress, and second, take action to minimize the potential and actual stressors in the workplace. This chapter looks at the support you can provide for employees.

Let's assume that you have spoken to the stressed employee and you now have an idea, vague or specific, about the degree of his distress and its possible causes within the workplace or outside. What can you do to support the employee yourself, and what resources are available within the organization to assist you?

Answering the following questions will provide you with an indication of what exists already and what you might need to do yourself:

- What welfare support do you have within your organization?
- What access is there, if any, to professional counselling for employees?
- What control do you, personally, have over the working conditions of your staff?

Given that the employee has talked to you about the situation, and that together you have identified at least some of the stressors involved, there are three possibilities concerning the origins of the stress and which determine the type of support you can offer:

- The stressors are personal.
- The stressors are work-based.
- They are a combination of both.

Supporting employees yourself means giving them your time, your attention and the space to explore issues to resolve difficulties. Where you have agreed action plans, support is about monitoring and reviewing the situation with the employees on a regular basis, discussing ensuing issues and providing the encouragement for them to take action or make changes themselves.

Personal stressors

If the stressors are purely personal, it is not your role to take action to reduce or remove them. However, this doesn't mean there is nothing you can do to support employees in the workplace. Your support may be crucial in keeping them at work or in reducing the effect of their personal problems on their work. Such support can be in the form of providing them time to talk about their situation and how you can help them while they are at work. It could mean referring them to a welfare officer, if you have one. Not only can the welfare workers provide a listening ear, but they may be able to provide information to enable employees to help themselves by, for example, providing leaflets about benefits or self-help groups. If you have a counselling service, you can provide employees with information about access to the service should they wish. Where no welfare service is available, the support will have to come directly from you or an outside agency. Your local Citizens Advice Bureau or local Council for Voluntary Service usually keep lists of organizations which provide help, support and self-help.

But there are other things you might be able to do as a

manager. The effects of relationship problems, financial problems, caring for dependants and other personal situations may mean the employee would benefit from being given a short time off, or a reduction in working hours for a temporary period, or being allowed to come in late or go home early. A flexible manager will see the benefits of relieving the pressure on the individual on a temporary basis. The loss in hours to the employer is likely to be no greater than the amount of ineffective time spent at work when the employee's attention and concerns are elsewhere. But don't assume *you* have the perfect answer! Talk to the employee to see how he thinks you might be able to help. See it as an investment in the employee concerned; an investment reaps later dividends. The employee's commitment to work will be enhanced if he knows you are genuinely trying to help.

Inevitably, there will always be employees who take advantage of any situation. But they are not the majority. Most employees are hard-working, committed and concerned, and deserve your time and effort.

A long-term problem will need a long-term solution. If the temporary support continues longer than you feel able to allow given the exigencies of the service, discuss long-term possibilities: permanent reduction in hours; job sharing; altering the working day.

There are solutions to most problems if only we are flexible and creative enough to be open to them.

Workplace stressors

If, in your discussions with distressed employees, they reveal workplace stressors, your role as a manager will be to investigate the situation and where possible take action. You may be expected to be able to *foresee* (see Chapter 2) likely consequences of the stress continuing. At the same time, distressed employees need your support.

To begin with, help is needed in exploring with the employees the details about the stressors and possible ways of overcoming them. Sometimes it may be a question of helping them come to terms with a change in their work patterns or a new project. Whatever the situation, they need to be supported throughout their period of distress, and their situation needs to be monitored carefully.

Remember, whether you believe there is any foundation or not to the existence of the workplace stressor, the employee still needs your help.

Be careful not to make a judgement either way about the existence of the stressor before you have investigated it. Yet remember that the distress felt by the employee is real. Many managers react against an employee who may be telling them things that they find uncomfortable or would rather not deal with (eg harassment by a trusted colleague of theirs). But ignoring an employee's distress because the manager didn't believe the story could be considered to be negligent.

It may be the situation that you are the cause of a person's distress, and in this case you may not be in the best position to deal with it unemotionally and objectively. This does not, however, mean that you can absolve yourself of your role in supporting and taking action. Rather it means working with another manager who can support the employee and act as a mediator between you.

Again, you can offer employees the support of the welfare worker, or, if appropriate, a counselling service (see below). If the perceived workplace stressor *is* a figment of their imagination or a distortion of reality, counselling may help them alter their perspective, and may unearth other issues which may be the root cause of the problem.

Welfare support

The welfare role has often been the Cinderella of the occupational health or personnel function in organizations. It has often been perceived as the optional extra. 'If the budgets allow, we'll do what we can' is a common response to the plea for employee support. Thus, while most organizations have a number of well-qualified safety officers, this is not matched by a comparable number of trained welfare staff.

Perhaps your company has one or two paid welfare officers, depending on its size. It will usually be their full-time responsibility to deal with any employee problems from financial to housing to personal issues to workplace problems. They are usually overworked, undervalued and underpaid. If the organization is a large one, the welfare workers may be supported by unpaid designated officers covering departments or work areas.

If you're unlucky, you have sole responsibility! However, there are outside agencies which may be able to provide information or support depending on the particular stressors, eg the Citizens Advice Bureau, Housing Advice Centres, Law Centres, Relate and other voluntary bodies.

But it is not a costly exercise for an organization to improve on its welfare provision. Managers are often highly paid professionals who have, in their managerial role, several different functions which they are expected to perform to a high degree of success. Managing the staff is one of the major functions as I have already highlighted. However, it would cost organizations less to appoint designated members of staff for the specific role of welfare support, thus relieving managers of the pressure, while offering a more impartial, confidential support for employees. These staff need to be empathetic, non-judgemental, to have integrity and commitment. They also need to be trained in listening skills. Employees should be able to approach these welfare staff of their own volition, or on the recommendation of their managers.

One issue for managers and welfare staff is *confidentiality*. It is a crucial issue, and one which often brings managers into conflict with welfare workers. Employees should have the right to disclose issues to welfare workers in a confidential situation. (The only exceptions, governed by reason, common sense and counselling code of ethics, is where the person is perceived to be a danger to themselves or to others.) Managers do *not* have a right to know. Some may wish they had; some believe that anything that occurs in the workplace is 'owned' by them; some may feel threatened by not knowing. But if you genuinely want to increase the effectiveness of your staff and to support them, you will understand the need for confidentiality. Trust is established as part of the culture, and you will actually learn more from a position of trust than from one of insisting on knowing. The latter culture engenders distrust, a lack of openness, and a reluctance to seek help. It is counterproductive to the efficiency of the whole organization to insist on a right to know. Furthermore, if an employee wishes to maintain confidentiality, you will not be deemed to have been able to foresee any deterioration in their mental health. So confidentiality can work to your advantage.

Professional counselling

There will always be a need for employees to have access to professional counselling, however comprehensive a welfare system your organization has. This can come in many different forms, from the in-house professional counsellor to a full employee assistance programme. Before we go into the pros and cons of different systems, let's briefly look at why professional counselling is needed.

The welfare officer has a distinct role from the counsellor, though some may talk of 'counselling' employees. It is a term which is often misused. The welfare officer deals with a range of practical, financial, procedural and health-based issues, but should be thought of as a short-term helper. Where employees need long-term help, where they have been damaged by experiences either in their past or currently, where they are seeking medical help for their mental health, they have moved beyond the help of the welfare worker. Some welfare workers believe they can deal with such issues. Without the qualifications and experience required for accreditation by the British Association for Counselling or the British Psychological Society (Chartered status), those believing they can counsel may well do more harm than good.

A good welfare officer, like a good manager, knows when employee problems are beyond them, when to refer, and when those who are professionally qualified should be made available.

And at this stage, it is worth reiterating that when I write about counselling being made available, I don't mean compulsorily. *Counselling can only ever be offered.* No employees will benefit from being forced to go to a counsellor, even if everyone thinks it's in their best interest for them to do so. People will only benefit from counselling if:

- they perceive they have a need for counselling;
- they want help.

Counselling covers a range of needs, from distress caused by marriage breakdown, sexual abuse, problems of or with adolescents, drug abuse, alcoholism, bereavement, workplace bullying to a range of stressors in between.

Again, at this point it is useful to remember that even when stressors emanate from people's private lives, stress has a knock-on effect in the workplace. Time and money invested in supporting an employee through personal crises will be well spent in terms of increased effectiveness at work.

So what are the alternatives in providing counselling at work?

In-house counsellors

In-house counsellors may have the advantage of knowing the workplace well and therefore understanding the workplace stressors. But they may also be perceived as part of the management structure of the organization and therefore distrusted by some employees. This can either be because of the employee's previous experience with 'management' or maybe because the employee concerned is part of that management and cannot be seen to be 'failing'.

Access to an in-house counsellor can also be problematic. How do you ensure confidentiality? Can the counselling venue be sited away from the workplace?

Are counsellors seen as a management tool by managers? Because they are directly employed by the company, will pressure be brought to bear on them to divulge confidences? One example may be in the case of an employee being disciplined, or one who has had 'too much' sick leave. If the counsellors are part of the management team, brought in perhaps to address workplace issues, will this be seen as compromising for their potential clients?

Are their services available to all employees? This is an important aspect for protecting the organization in litigation cases. Unless counselling is available equally to all employees, litigation may still be a real prospect in relation to employees who are denied opportunities to receive professional help.

Sessional counselling

External counselling can be bought on an hourly basis. The costs for professional counsellors range from £30 to £80 and upwards per hour depending on geographic location and other factors personal to the individual counsellor. This cost makes it almost prohibitive to offer sessional counselling comprehensively to all employees needing help.

If access is selective, what criteria are to be used to allocate sessions? Worth to the organization? Seniority? Mental health need? And who selects? The manager? The welfare worker?

And what of the employees who feel vulnerable, who are worried about admitting their inability to cope? What access do they have?

Again, if the sessional counselling is not available to all employees, it cannot be used as a protection for the company from litigation.

Tele-counselling

Tele-counselling is a full counselling service in which clients are counselled by telephone only. The advantages are that confidentiality can be fully guaranteed, and for this reason it is often favoured by senior managers. It is also more easily accessible by those who have difficulties in accessing buildings or who lack transport or who are too ill to leave home.

Tele-counselling can be provided for a whole company at reasonable costs because it doesn't require premises or major overheads. And, because it is comprehensive, it can therefore provide statistical information on workplace stressors to enable the company to address issues internally.

The main disadvantage is that many people are not comfortable with using telephones, many do not have access to telephones where they can talk in confidence, and the benefits to both client and counsellor of non-verbal communication are lost.

Partial employee assistance programme

An employee assistance programme (EAP) is a comprehensive, confidential counselling system usually provided by an external organization, and is costed either on a per use basis or a fixed per capita annual amount.

A *partial* EAP is actually a contradiction in terms since one of the main features of an employee assistance programme is its comprehensiveness. However, where an organization is separated into distinct groups, departments or geographic locations, and where there are financial barriers to implementing a full programme, an employee assistance programme can serve a defined group. In terms of litigation, the company would only be protected for that part of the organization.

A partial programme could be used where certain workers are more vulnerable to stress because of the nature of their work. Such an example is the social services department of a local authority.

The disadvantage of this model for a company is that while some groups might be more vulnerable as a group, individual differences between groups may be costing the employer more in terms of ineffectiveness and inefficiency. The advantages of any employee assistance programme are outlined below.

Full employee assistance programme

Employee assistance programmes come in as many different forms as there are providers. Each will offer a comprehensive, confidential counselling service for all employees including a dedicated telephone line, and external venues for one-to-one counselling. Costs for an EAP can vary widely, and organizations may be offered two options on cost: a fixed annual fee based on the number of employees who are entitled to access the programme, or a per use fee.

It is up to the individual purchasing organization to specify what they require from the programme, and therefore an EAP does not have to be extortionate in financial terms. Many EAP packages offered are 'off the peg', and include publicity, training and other services such as financial or legal services. Obviously, the more services required, the higher the per capita cost. Many of these services can be provided in-house in a more cost-effective way. It would be up to the organization to negotiate an appropriate package for its needs and circumstances.

One of the main benefits of the external EAP is that it is separate from the purchasing company and therefore is seen by employees to be independent and impartial. This means that more employees will use the service because they have confidence in it. This is a positive benefit to the organization where it has chosen to pay a fixed annual fee rather than a per use fee.

Besides providing counselling support for distressed employees, an EAP should also provide general statistics which, while protecting individual confidentiality, can identify major workplace stressors for internal action by the purchasing organization. In this way, an EAP could save an organization money in the long term if that organization is willing to address the issues arising.

EAPs will usually only take referrals from employees themselves. This is on the basis that employees will only benefit if they wish to have counselling. Many managers find it threatening that employees can go to an external agency, divulge problems about the workplace which they, as managers, might not know about.

One or two reassurances are necessary here. First, if employees want their manager to take action to reduce or remove a stressor, they may break their own confidentiality after discussing the issues with a counsellor. Second, if there is no indication in an employee's behaviour or work that something is wrong, what benefit would there be to that manager in knowing anything? If the employee wishes the issue to remain confidential, this protects the employer because any subsequent issues are not *foreseeable*. Sometimes there are benefits in not knowing! A counsellor will never undermine a manager's right to manage. Indeed, the counselling service is there to underpin the manager's role, to support the employee and to identify workplace issues.

Suffice to say that a good manager has never felt threatened by confidential counselling!

Choosing the best option

So of all the options, which is the best?

To support the employee, and to provide protection for the employer, any counselling should:

- be available and accessible to *all* employees;
- be confidential;
- be independent and impartial;
- only utilize fully qualified and experienced counsellors;
- provide statistical feedback on stressors within the workplace.

Nevertheless, as a manager you may have little influence on which option your organization utilizes. Where an organization has no counselling service available, you may feel you wish to raise this at a senior level, at least to point out that the organization is not only leaving itself wide open to future compensation claims, but may be costing itself more expenditure in terms of sickness absence. In addition, you as a manager need to have your efforts underpinned to be totally effective.

Easing a return to work

Let us now return to the situation where one of your employees is off work, you have provided him with appropriate support, and have addressed any workplace issues. How can you then enable him to return to work as a fully effective member of your team?

Many employees who have found it necessary to take sick

leave for reasons of stress are away from work for some weeks. Where there is no professional support offered or available, the length of the sickness absence is likely to be greater. Either way, the thought of returning to work after a long absence is stressful in itself. (Think of how you feel after a two-week holiday!) In these circumstances, employees might benefit from a staggered return, such as a few weeks of half days, or coming in later and going home earlier. Although the organization may wish the return to be absolute, a flexible approach will yield better returns. Many employees who return after a lengthy absence find they are unable to cope with a full week's work, and if this is insisted upon it may result in regression and further sickness absence.

If there is no alternative to a full return to work, managers could look at lightening the workload for a few weeks, or providing extra help. Bear in mind that if you are aware of the underlying reasons for the ill health and you fail to take action which might improve the employee's wellbeing, you may be deemed to be negligent or culpable at a later time.

There are obviously workplace issues which need to be discussed and agreed with the employee *before the return to work*. Indeed, some general practitioners will not issue final medical certificates until they are assured that their patients' needs are accommodated in some way.

The more sceptical managers among you may be feeling that this is a soft option, a 'whinger's charter'. However, if you think of it from a financial perspective, it is, again, an investment in an organization's valuable resources which will provide greater returns in the future. As with all investments, there is an element of risk.

No organization has ever achieved greatness without taking some risks!

Summary

- Employees need to be supported when they are experiencing stress.
- This support can be from the manager, welfare worker, professional counsellor, or all three.
- Whether the stressor is real or imagined, the employee needs support.
- Managers should discuss flexible working arrangements with stressed employees to enable them to remain at work.
- To protect an organization in litigation cases, counselling should be available to all.
- Managers need to be flexible in enabling an employee's effective return to work after stress-related sickness.

Exercises

1. Find out what support services are available in your organization.
2. If there are none, find out what services agencies in the community offer.
3. Think about the different ways you can support employees to prevent them needing to take time off work, or to ease their return to work.
4. Seek guidance from your senior managers about their attitude to flexible solutions.
5. Make enquiries of companies who provide EAPs so that you can assess the cost and possible savings for your organization.

CHAPTER 7
Preventing or Reducing Stress at Work

In the last chapter we discussed ways of directly supporting the employee who is experiencing difficulties. In this chapter, we will go one stage further and look at the different ways in which you, in your role as manager, can work with employees to reduce or eliminate stressors in the work situation.

Chapter 8 provides a detailed checklist or inventory of all those areas which are known to cause stress at work, in the form of questions. The list is not prescriptive in any way, and the more creatively it is used, the more successful you are likely to be in dealing with the stressors.

However, before looking at the detailed checklist, it is useful to consider the key areas where stress occurs, and to think about actions that can be taken to improve the effectiveness of *every employee* at work. The key areas are:

- the culture of the organization;
- the environment in which people work;
- people;
- the job itself;
- opportunities for development;
- the management of change.

The culture of the organization

The culture of the organization emanates from the top, and percolates through the organization by means of the management structure, its methods of communication, its predominant management styles, its policies and practices. Though individual managers may be at odds with the prevailing culture, it is a powerful animal, and will be felt and understood by employees at every level whether positively or negatively.

However, there is much that individual managers can do to influence the culture of their own part of the organization (without causing waves) by considering the elements which employees find stressful. If you go back to the list of stressors on page 27 and note all those potential stressors which can be subsumed under the heading of culture, you will find that employees are concerned about:

- lack of communication;
- lack of consultation;
- autocratic management style;
- lack of trust;
- lack of participation;
- too many rules;
- attitudes to absence, capability and discipline.

These are all areas which you, as a manager, can influence. You can:

- hold regular team meetings;
- welcome comments from all staff;
- involve your team in the organization of the work;
- develop informal lines of communication;
- have an open door policy;
- use existing policies and procedures sensitively and with discretion.

All these actions will make your staff feel valued, and will increase their commitment. Being heavy-handed may have the opposite effect. To take one example, draconian measures to control sickness absence are often counter-productive, resulting in increasing stress levels and ineffectiveness at work. Looking at underlying causes and dealing with them appropriately will, in the long term, pay dividends *and* reduce the absence figures.

Empowering employees, giving them a feeling of belonging and of having something to offer, will increase their effectiveness; it will not lead to a watering-down of your sphere of influence, as some managers fear. If you're sceptical, or if this style of management is alien to you, give it a try, talk to managers who already use these methods, or look at some of the published material in this field.

The environment in which people work

The physical environment in which employees spend some forty hours a week plays an important part in their effectiveness during those hours. While health and safety regulations require you to reduce the risk of damage from toxic substances, gases, noise, VDU work and much more, there are many other physical influences which are detrimental to an employee's emotional wellbeing and which are inexpensive to improve. Remember, employers have a responsibility under health and safety legislation for this.

If you have an open style of management, then you will already welcome suggestions from employees about improving their working conditions. The employees, after all, are the people who know how they feel about the office they work in, the condition of the shop floor, the discomforts of the machinery they work with, their lack of privacy. Talk to your team about their working environment, and listen to their suggestions. *Don't assume that you know what is best for them.* You are not inviting complaints, you are inviting suggestions for improvements.

These improvements may range from the minor to the major. Even minor improvements like adding plants or pictures, moving furniture around, or resiting screens, cost little, but can make a dismal office into something more user friendly. You only have to look at individual desks to see how some employees improve their micro environment with a plant, a photo or an ornament. Forty hours in a work setting is longer than most of us spend awake in our homes. And think of all the (often inexpensive) improvements we make to have better living conditions at home. All of us work better in an environment in which we feel comfortable. Obviously we all have different tastes, but compromise is one of the keys to effective team working.

People

People, as we discussed earlier, are the biggest stressors in the workplace whether they are the managing directors, team leaders, colleagues or subordinates. It is not within your power to control all your team members, however much you might like to! But you can take effective action to ensure that difficulties caused between people are dealt with, and dealt with immediately and sensitively.

Unfair treatment, bullying, unreasonable behaviour, harassment, aggression, and personality conflicts are all inappropriate in a workplace setting (or anywhere else), but they are common and they are stressful both to experience and to deal with.

Unfair treatment is often illegal and is most often covered by an organization's equal opportunities policies which frequently go beyond the law. However, even in organizations with enlightened policies, unfairness does take place. If sanctioned, albeit by default, employees will not trust the organization. They will not trust it to appoint or promote the best person; they will not trust it to value what they have to offer objectively; they will feel unsure of how they are perceived by those in control. And with lack of trust comes lack of commitment.

Harassment, which includes bullying, aggression, conflict of personalities, unreasonable behaviour, assault, misuse of power, and a whole host of other detrimental actions by one or more persons against another, is the greatest stressor of them all. And it is the one area of work that managers most hate to deal with. If they can sweep it under the carpet, they will. But such an attitude is not only counter-productive from an organizational point of view, it could well be considered *negligent*.

If your company does not have a policy for dealing with harassment, you will need to find your own method of doing so. And the first thing to do is to talk to the complainants concerned, in confidence, to find out what and whose behaviour is causing offence or disquiet. If you have investigating officers who can, with some degree of objectivity, investigate complaints, so much the better. If not, you need to ask yourself, are you the best person to deal with this? Can you be objective enough? Are you involved?

At the end of the day, dealing with most day to day forms of harassment should be less about apportioning blame than ensuring that it stops and supporting the employee being harassed. This book is not about harassment, although it could well be. If there is no clear policy in your organization for dealing with it, you may need to get outside help or refer to experts.

The message here is: deal with issues between people and deal with them immediately.

The job itself

When people accept a job, they usually have an idea of what is expected of them in their role. They may have a job description, an employee specification, terms and conditions of employment and information gleaned from an interview. But frequently, once in the job, things can begin to alter almost imperceptibly or even change drastically. For example, the work load is varied, the tasks become automated, the hours are extended, the line of reporting is changed, the role is unclear. The employees themselves may have altered their views: the shift work becomes onerous, the travelling excessive, the work boring and repetitive, the technology too demanding.

Your role as a manager is to ensure that the exigencies of the organization are met. But without the commitment of the employees, you cannot achieve your goals. If the employees are unhappy, it will be reflected in their work output.

Effective communication is the key to ensuring you know when an employee is unhappy with a fundamental aspect of their work. An open door policy might not be sufficient here. The employee may quietly be thinking that the job is no longer the right one for them; they may be feeling confused, undermined, undervalued. And they are likely to keep such thoughts to themselves. They may look for another job, in which case you have the potential expense of recruitment and retraining and a loss of expertise, or they may become less effective, which equally has a hidden cost.

However, if you have a regular review time with each employee on a one-to-one basis, this is the ideal opportunity to bring out such thoughts and feelings. With such a system, provided it can be flexible, employees will not feel you are singling them out for personal reasons. Together you can clarify roles and responsibilities, lines of reporting and any difficulties arising. And once you have established that a difficulty or problem exists, then is the time to explore options. Again, as emphasized throughout, never assume you know what is best to resolve other people's problems. Ask them, be open to suggestions and offer your own. Compromise is a skill worth developing.

Such review meetings should be no less frequent than six monthly. If they are reinforced by a genuine open door policy, you are likely to be able to deal with any potentially damaging issues at the earliest stage before the employee or the organization suffers.

Opportunities for development

Few people ever reach their full potential. It is in an organization's interest to give its employees every opportunity to maximize that potential. The company will be the beneficiary in the long term through increased motivation and commitment, increased productivity and the best use of resources. However, many organizations, particularly under pressure of limited finance, do not view training and development as an investment for themselves. Rather, it seems to be a useful budget head when savings have to be made.

To begin with, employees need the tools for the job. You may be providing them with the word processor, but are you giving them the training they need to maximize the use of the processor? Are you providing your newly appointed supervisors or managers with the skills they need to get the best out of their staff? If you've introduced a new method of working, have you told the employees? Have you provided them with the opportunities they need to gain experience of the new methods?

If employees are trained and developed, if their managers talk to them about their personal needs and practical requirements for performing their duties, and for their future development, then the employees will feel valued, will feel of worth to the company, and will repay the investment with interest.

An undervalued employee is usually an unhappy one who, in the immediate future, is going to feel less and less motivated, less efficient and, in extreme cases (not unknown in the world of commerce), subversive and destructive.

The half-yearly review meeting with each employee is an ideal opportunity for discussing personal development needs. And training and development opportunities don't have to mean spending vast amounts of money. There may be local courses, discussion groups, colleague help, mentoring, whole team meetings, correspondence courses and many other ways of fulfilling need. As with any good management, it requires a flexible and creative approach to maximize the outcome for all parties.

The management of change

Any form of change in our lives causes us some degree of stress initially. We all have to learn to adjust to the myriad of changes that affect us both in our personal lives and in the workplace. The majority of us do this adequately, and though we might not welcome the change, we adapt to it. Others are less easily adaptable and may suffer greatly through imposed changes, and may, intentionally or inadvertently, sabotage the positive benefits of the change

However, the negative effects of any change can be reduced by those who have some control over the process of change provided they are aware of the reasons for people's fear and reticence. If we initiate change ourselves, or if we are part of a body of people responsible for introducing change into the workplace, we can minimize the negative effects by managing the process at all stages from the pre-change to post-change situation. This may require more time in which to implement the changes, but in the longer term it ensures that the change is more readily accepted and adopted by participants.

The key requirements to successfully implementing change are:

- time;
- information;
- consultation and participation;
- support.

First, those involved in the proposed change, however remotely, need to be *informed* fully of what the changes are, what the implications are for their work, and the reasons for their proposal. Where possible, the consultation process should include all those involved to ensure their commitment and acceptance of the change. Where this is not possible, as much information as possible should be provided on the benefits of the change to the organization, its customers, and to its employees.

Second, employees need *time* to absorb the proposals, to adjust to the changes, to formulate their thoughts, to air their views. A rashly implemented process of change is doomed to failure. Change agents should be able to anticipate the effects on their employees and to have thought through strategies for responding to fears, worries, and complaints.

Where employees are *consulted* before changes become tablets of stone, and where that consultation process is genuine, the process of change runs much more smoothly and quickly. Seeking solutions to problems from those who are closest to them (often the employees at ground level) is an excellent way of ensuring their involvement in its successful implementation: they have a stake in its success. Equally, in situations where the implementation process is less than smooth, consultation may result in the change process being firmly back on course.

Lastly, all participants in the process of change need to know that they will be *supported* through the process. Sometimes this will just mean that their views are sought, their worries listened to and answered; at other times, they may need to talk to the manager on a one to one basis for reassurance, to ask for additional training, to express their fears on a personal basis.

Good managers will anticipate the worries of the employee where change is proposed and, where they are not a change agent themselves, but merely the bringer of bad tidings (as is sometimes the case) they can nevertheless do all in their power to minimize the negative effects using the above strategies. Lack of power and involvement should not inhibit good management practice.

Summary

- Preventing and reducing stress is not a costly exercise.
- Give employees the opportunity to influence their work situation.
- Hold regular informal meetings.
- Ensure equality of opportunity.
- Deal with interpersonal conflicts immediately and efficiently.
- Hold regular review meetings to discuss work roles and development needs.
- Where change is proposed, the negative effects can be minimized by providing information, time, consultation, and support for employees.

Exercises

1. For each of the areas of potential stress identified above, make a note of those which you can improve:
   - at no cost;
   - at little cost;
   - with the agreement of your superiors.
2. Prioritize the areas in which you need to take action.
3. Start working through these priorities.
4. Review your progress at regular intervals.

CHAPTER 8
The Workplace Stress Inventory

This checklist or inventory is intended to alert managers to the possible stressors existing within their work arenas and, without being prescriptive, to encourage managers to take some action to remove or reduce the potential stressors. It can therefore be used both a diagnostic tool and as a preventative measure.

Individual response

Your response to its content must necessarily be an individual one dependent on the type of organization you work for, its prevailing culture, the power and control you have as a manager, and, of course, your own views and philosophies on management.

What is important is that you *take action* where you know that something is wrong. To do otherwise is to be *negligent*. Using the checklist, you can go one step further and *prevent* things going wrong in the first place.

At the end of this chapter, you will find suggestions of different ways in which you can use the inventory to improve your work area. As you read through the inventory you may have already formed ideas about ways in which it would be appropriate to use it in your work environment and with your style of management.

1. The culture of the organization

a) What methods of formal communication exist between employer and employees, and between you as manager and your employees?
- Are they adequate?
- Are they two-way?
- Have you consulted staff about the effectiveness of communication?
- Do you hold regular staff meetings?
- Do you operate an 'open-door' policy?

b) Are staff consulted in matters relating to them?
- Is there a staff consultative process?
- Is membership of a trade union welcomed?
- Do you consult your employees about work issues?
- Do you welcome suggestions for improvements?

c) What is the prevailing management style of the organization?
- Are employees empowered by the organization?
- Do you involve your staff in team decisions?

d) How are you expected to operate the rules of the organization?
- Does the system allow for flexibility?
- Do you give employees the opportunity to discuss difficulties?

e) Does the organization have an equal opportunities policy?
- Are all employees made aware of the policy?
- How are employees who use this policy perceived by the organization?
- Are complainants protected from victimization?
- Is contravention of the policy treated seriously?
- Is your own practice fair?

2. The environment in which people work

a) Are the following hazards controlled and regulated to ensure employees' comfort and safety?
- Temperature?
- Noise?
- Lighting?
- Ventilation?
- Vibration?
- Exposure to toxic substances, chemicals, dusts, gases, fumes?

b) Are the conditions of buildings and offices:
- Overcrowded?
- Untidy?
- Clean?
- Drab?

c) Is the layout of the workplace:
- Too small?
- Overcrowded?
- Isolated?
- Lacking privacy?
- Well-planned for its use?

d) Are the staff facilities adequate and/or well kept?
- Toilet areas?
- Rest rooms?
- Designated smoking areas?
- Refreshment facilities?
- Confidential rooms?

e) Is the machinery or equipment
- Sited appropriately?
- Suitable for the specified job?
- Designed with the user in mind?
- In good condition?
- Maintained and serviced regularly?
- Safe?

3. People
  a) What is your relationship with your staff like?
  - Are you considerate?
  - Are you perceived to be fair?
  - Do you trust and respect your employees?
  - Do you think they trust and respect you?
  - Have you received formal management training?
  - Do you encourage participation in work decisions?
  - Do you delegate appropriately?
  - Do you provide regular feedback to all employees?
  - Do you show you value your employees? How?
  - Do you say 'thank you' to your team members?
  - Have you assessed your own stress level and taken action to reduce it?
  - Do you know your staff well enough to recognize when they might be stressed?

  b) What are relationships between team members like?
  - Is there co-operation between colleagues, and do you encourage this?
  - Do team members trust and support each other?
  - Are you aware of what behaviour constitutes harassment and your responsibilities in relation to these?
  - Do you take measures to ensure harassment does not take place?
  - How do you deal with personality clashes?

  c) What is your own relationship with your manager/s?
  - Are your lines of management clear?
  - Are you given the support you need?
  - Are you consulted in matters relating to your management area?
  - Do you approach your manager on behalf of your staff?
  - Can you approach your manager for your own developmental needs?

  d) How do you deal with employees who are causing concern in the workplace?

- Do you give them an opportunity to talk about issues in confidence?
- Do you offer them confidential support?
- Do you take action on issues they raise?
- Are you flexible in taking steps to support them through a process of recovery or improvement?

4. The job itself

a) Is the job of each of your members of staff stimulating enough?
- Is there enough variety in the tasks?
- Are all the tasks boring, repetitive or arduous?
- Does the job make few demands on the employee?
- Is all the work unskilled?
- Are enough breaks offered?
- Can the job be redesigned to provide more variety?

b) Is the amount of work satisfactory?
- Is there too much for one person?
- Are your expectations too high?
- Have you enough staff for the tasks in hand?
- Are the staff adequately trained to fulfil the tasks?
- Can extra help be provided for peaks?
- Do employees have any control over how and when they perform the tasks?
- Can extra projects be provided during troughs?
- Is the work mentally overloading?
- If the work involves stressed or potentially violent clients or customers, is adequate support and training provided?

c) Are the job arrangements adequate?
- Are travel requirements excessive?
- Have family circumstances been taken into account?
- Have employees been consulted where locations are altered?
- Are the hours unsociable?
- Are you aware of the stresses of shift work?
- Do you operate shift systems flexibly?

- Can you alter rotas to take account of employee needs?
- Is the machinery/technology suitable for the employee?
- Are adequate breaks given for VDU operators, employees whose job entails standing, or where work is physically demanding?

d) Are the roles of the job clear?
- Is the employee aware of the duties required?
- Do you provide regular opportunities to discuss roles?
- Have you communicated your expectations clearly?
- Where there is role conflict, do you take action to minimize this?
- Are you consistent in your level of expectation?
- Is the level of given responsibility reasonable for the incumbent?
- Is enough time provided for staff with responsibilities for others to fulfil their managerial roles?

e) Are exit interviews provided so that the organization can rectify any shortcomings?
- When employees leave do you offer them the opportunity to talk to you in confidence about their reasons for leaving?
- Do you act on the information you receive in this way?

5. Opportunities for development
a) Does the organization value its employees by providing training and development opportunities?
- Does the organization have a formal mechanism for reviewing staff development and training needs?
- Is training and development offered to all employees regardless of level, status and hours of work?
- Do you encourage your staff to take promotional or developmental opportunities?
- Do you discuss training and development outcomes with employees?
- Do you provide opportunities for staff to put new learning into practice or to cascade information gained?

b) Is equality of opportunity adhered to in developmental matters?

- Do you ensure that training, developmental opportunities and special projects are offered fairly?
- Are all promotional opportunities and vacancies advertised fairly?
- Are employees encouraged to pursue qualification courses, supported financially and given reasonable time off work for this purpose?

6. Implementing change

- Have employees been consulted at all stages of the process?
- Is information freely available in a range of formats (meetings, newsletters, seminars, memos, etc)?
- Has plenty of time been allowed for assimilation of proposals and their possible effects?
- Have you offered individual support to employees affected by the change?
- Is support available throughout the process of change and beyond?

Possible ways of using the inventory to improve the workplace

The inventory can be used in a number of ways to achieve the same ends: reducing the number of stressors in the workplace. You may have your own ideas of how you can adapt the inventory and use it for your own particular workplace. Or you could use it:

- as a thorough exercise in assessing the risk of stress and identifying potential stressors in your area of control. You could assign numerical values to the different risks and their possible effects;
- to help you pinpoint particular issues which need addressing when employees have raised concerns;
- as a preparation for staff development/appraisal meetings;

- as an agenda item on staff meetings to involve whole teams on improving the workplace;
- as a team-building exercise.

CHAPTER 9
Managing Employee Stress: Case Studies

This chapter is intended to give you the opportunity to put into practice all the aspects of managing stress we have covered in the previous chapters using case studies.

Before you attempt the case studies, however, it will be useful to reiterate the main points of the guide and the manager's role in relation to stress in the workplace. These are:

- Employers have a responsibility under health and safety legislation for the mental wellbeing of their employees at work.
- The effects of stress are costly and damaging if the issues are not dealt with at an early stage.
- Every manager needs to be aware of the causes, effects and symptoms of stress.
- If managers know their staff well, they will be able to recognize the signs of stress in employees and take early effective action to minimize the impact on the individual and the workplace.
- A manager needs to develop good listening skills to enhance the process of communication.
- Managers should not assume that they know what is best for an employee.

- A stressed employee needs to be supported by the manager at every stage, including the return to work after any sickness absence.
- Where underlying causes of stress in the workplace are known, these should be dealt with; lack of finance is not a legitimate excuse for inaction.
- Managers should assess the risk of stress in their work area to reduce or minimize its existence; a checklist can enhance this process.
- A flexible approach in managing employees under stress is beneficial to both the employee and the organization.
- A confidential counselling service which is available to all employees will support damaged employees and increase an organization's protection against litigation.

Using the case studies

The following case studies are examples of the types of problem managers may face in their day to day work. It is intended that as you read them, you can assume the role as the subject's manager, and think about how you might respond in such a situation. A series of questions then follow which are designed to alert you to the different aspects of the situation and to help you frame your response. This is then followed by a discussion of how a manager might deal with such a situation. Obviously an individual manager will respond in relation to his or her own work situation, and therefore the discussion is not offered as *the right way* but as *one way* of responding, and is provided as a comparison with your own response.

The case studies can be used on an individual basis by a manager reading this guide, or they can be used in teams where participants pool ideas. This latter approach is a useful exercise since we are all restricted by our own perspectives. Listening to other people's points of view increases our understanding and enhances our ability to be more flexible in how we deal with situations.

Case Study 1

Background
Jane has been a valued member of your team for over five years. You feel you know her well. She is reliable and hard-working and has never let you down. She is married and has two school-age children. She travels twenty miles to work each day, and has never been late. You promoted her two years ago, and have been pleased with her work. Recently she told you she was thinking of studying for a degree.

Situation
You have a policy of seeing each of your staff on a regular six-monthly basis to review their work and to discuss any developmental needs. At Jane's review session today, she breaks down in tears and tells you she can't cope any longer, and that she is overloaded.

Questions

1. Is it appropriate to continue with the discussion if she is very tearful?
2. Have you noticed any deterioration in her work or behaviour up to this point?
3. Who is the best person for her to talk to?
4. What support can you offer her?
5. What are the workplace issues?
6. How would you try to resolve them?
7. What documentation, if any, would you keep?
8. When and how might you review the situation?

These questions are not the only ones you need to consider. If you work through your own responses to this situation before you read the discussion below, you will probably be able to think of many more questions or issues that are relevant.

You can invent some of the details of her situation to make the study more realistic or perhaps more apposite to your own work area or experience. Be creative.

Discussion

1. Jane may or may not wish to continue with the discussion. It would be best to give her the option of deciding whether she would like to rearrange the interview when she is more composed. If she knows you well, she may not be embarrassed by her breakdown, but relieved to be able to talk to you. If she does want to rearrange the discussion, don't leave her to cry on her own. Ask her what you or anyone else can do to help her. She might just want a five-minute break, or space to recover. Let her determine the pace. If she wishes to rearrange, make a definite time and date as soon as possible, so that the issues will be dealt with.

2. You have obviously not noticed anything wrong. She may be good at covering up; the cause of her upset may have been very recent; it may be a personal situation rather than a work one. Whatever the cause, she has highlighted a problem for her – her inability to cope – and you now have a responsibility to deal with that aspect.

3. The chances are, you are the best person to talk to since she has raised the issue with you. However, give her the option. If the underlying cause is very personal she may not wish to off-load to you (you may be grateful for this). If you have a welfare service and counselling service, offer her these. Otherwise ask her who she would like to talk to. Nevertheless, you will still need to talk to her about the workload and coping.

4. Having offered her welfare support, counselling and your own listening ear, what more can you do? This will depend on the stressors. If there are personal problems, does she need time off to sort out any issues? Would coming in later or working from home relieve the burden for her? There are many more possibilities depending on her situation. Again, ask her what support she needs. If the stressors are in the workplace, you can discuss possibilities for support together.

5. There are two main presenting issues (as opposed to the

underlying ones): the not coping and the workload. Have you increased her workload recently? Has another member of staff left and not been replaced, thereby putting her under pressure? Explore with her the aspects of her workload and what you can do to help. If the workload has remained constant, why is she unable to cope now: what else is going on? Here you may uncover issues with other members of staff. By listening to her you will be able to tease out the issues. If the reason is her own current emotional state, maybe everything needs to be put on hold until she has counselling, or time away from work. Has she consulted her GP?

6. If she is overloaded with work, she needs more support, help with prioritizing, rescheduling of deadlines, fewer cases or projects, people to delegate to, less pressure from colleagues or perhaps other managers. Are there any developmental needs which aren't being met, and if so, can you rectify this? If other people at work are putting her under pressure, what is happening? Is there role conflict, unclear lines of responsibility, harassment? If so, investigate, clarify roles and responsibilities, end the harassment (see Case Study 3).

7. You probably keep some record of review meetings. Notes can be made on whatever you have agreed concerning her workload, with a clearly stated and agreed review process which should be much closer than the normal six-monthly review. It would probably be a breach of confidentiality to detail any personal problems Jane might have mentioned, but where you are allowing flexibility of workload or hours for such reasons, unspecified personal reasons can be mentioned.

8. You need to keep the situation with Jane under close surveillance to ensure she is receiving the help she needs. If she chooses not to see a counsellor, her GP or anyone else, that is up to her. But if she is still unable to cope you need to have regular meetings with her to support and encourage her, and to review what is happening. Be realistic in terms of time scale. If, for example, she is going

through a marriage break-up, this will be more long term in its effects than if she is nursing someone through a short-term illness. If her ability to cope increases, don't be too quick to add more work. Allow her to recover her equilibrium at a reasonable pace. Remember, she has always been reliable and hard-working in the past. It will cost much more in the long run to replace her and her years of expertise than to weather her temporary lack of effectiveness.

Case Study 2

Background

John is one of a team of labourers whose work you manage. He is well liked by the team members, and organizes social events for them. He has a grown-up family who all live close by. His wife is a cleaner with the company. He has worked for the company for several years. He is a gregarious man, always telling jokes and being the life and soul of the group.

Situation

You are walking through the canteen when you notice a small group of your team (all male) laughing and joking. John is among them, but, unusually, he is not participating. Only yesterday, the supervisor was muttering to you about the lack of team spirit among the men.

Questions

1. Do you bear these two apparently unrelated points in mind, or do you decide to do something about it now?
2. How would you approach John if he hasn't done anything wrong?
3. Are there any workplace issues here, and if so, what can you do about them?
4. Do you document any of your thoughts or actions?

Discussion

1. Before you take any action regarding John, you might wish to talk to the supervisor to find out whether the lack of team spirit is affecting the work in any way, or whether there has been any behaviour causing him concern. It would not be appropriate to mention John's name specifically; you would merely be trying to get some background information. If there is no problem from the supervisor's point of view, then you would be dealing with a situation which at present is just affecting John. It is worth approaching John casually at this stage to pre-empt the escalation of any problems for him or the company. If there is no problem, other than perhaps a momentary lack of exuberance or enthusiasm, you have not lost anything, and John will know that you care.

2. As you know John well, and if you have always had a good relationship with him, you might wish to catch him on his own and ask him if he could spare you a minute. Exactly how you do this would be a matter of custom and practice with this group: are they used to talking to you in your office, or in the canteen or somewhere else? Perhaps you sometimes have a drink with them, in which case is this an ideal opportunity? (Sometimes even a public place can be more confidential than somewhere in the workplace where other workers might read more into a meeting than there is.) When you get John on his own, then you can make a casual statement about him not seeming his normal self. He may open up or close up depending on what is going on for him (if anything). If he closes up, there is no harm in offering him a listening ear or support should he ever want it. You might ask after his family and his own health in passing. You are not being intrusive if you do not pursue this beyond the casual questions of a friend or colleague. Obviously, if you had been on bad terms with John, such questions would be inappropriate. If he opens up, you may unearth issues which require you to offer him support to overcome or weather, or which you need to take action on in the workplace.

3. To begin with, there don't seem to be any overt workplace issues, though John may reveal some. However, there is usually a reason for a lack of team spirit, particularly if it has been in evidence before, and this may have a detrimental effect on the team workings. If John doesn't reveal anything, you still need to be aware of something not being right, and you might wish to talk to the team as a whole (if, again, this is custom and practice) to get to the bottom of it. Maybe they have heard rumours about a lay-off, or a take-over? Maybe a newcomer has disrupted the comfortable workings of the group? Is communication between you and the group everything it should be? Are the workers involved enough in the work of the team? Are they being developed? It is easy to make assumptions about the development needs of unskilled or semi-skilled workers, but you may be very wrong. Talk to them as a group or singly. Whether or not anything is revealed, you need to monitor the team in terms of cohesion, work output, and team spirit to ensure that the supervisor's rumblings weren't the tip of the iceberg.

4. If the whole event seems to be a storm in a teacup, there is probably no point in documenting anything. If, however, John reveals issues that need following up in the workplace, this does need to be recorded, and reviewed. If the whole team raise issues arising from you opening up communication with them, then records of this should be documented. If you offer employees the opportunity to give their viewpoint, don't devalue them by doing nothing about it. At least come back to them with reasons why something can't be done.

To begin with, John's case seemed fairly straightforward and innocuous, but looking at possible developments, by taking early action you may have saved John from a downward spiral which might also have affected the rest of the team, or you may have saved the company from potential industrial action if disquiet had been brewing beneath the surface. And all you invested was an hour or so of your time with John, and perhaps a team meeting.

I am not advocating that you look for problems where they don't exist, but that you are sensitive to possibilities if you notice a change in behaviour or personality. We all have days when we feel down, and the last thing anyone wants is for managers to breathe down our necks every time they see us looking less than on top of the world. It is a question of balance and perspective.

Case Study 3

Background
One of the teams you manage is the clerical support staff: a team of three women and two young men who are supervised by Mary. Mary has been with you for two years, and generally you leave her to manage the team on a day to day basis. However, you have daily contact with the support staff. You find Mary to be reliable, and the other teams never complain about the work of her team. Although you don't know her very well, she always seems pleasant and friendly.

Situation
Today, one of the clerical workers, Sandy, asks to see you in confidence. She tells you that she can't take any more hassle from Mary, and that she has been picking on her for months. Now she dreads coming to work, and has had a number of days' sickness with migraine. She is thinking of leaving, but doesn't see why Mary should force her out.

Questions
1. How do you handle the meeting with Sandy?
2. Do you take her word for what is happening?
3. How confidential is the disclosure by Sandy?
4. What are the workplace issues and how can you deal with them?
5. Do you have company policies to fall back on?
6. What issues are there around Sandy's sickness record?
7. What support can you offer and to whom?

8. What documentation do you need to keep?
9. How will you review the situation?

Discussion

1. Sandy has come to you voluntarily and in doing so obviously wants some help. You need to get the full story from her, though, before you can take any action. What are the instances of the hassle, how frequent, is it just with her or with any of the others, are there witnesses, how does Sandy feel, has she talked to anyone else ... if you give her the opportunity to open up, she is likely to give you the answers to these questions and many more. When the story is complete, you need to confirm the salient points with her to make sure you have got the story right. You then need to discuss options for further action. You have only heard Sandy's side of events, and you must therefore reserve judgement until you know more. However, Sandy needs to know that she has not come to you in vain. You might offer her support from a welfare officer, maybe the counselling service if you have one, and state that you will investigate the situation immediately. You might need to ask whether she is able to continue in the team at the moment, given that you are now aware and will keep an eye on things. If she is very distressed, you might think about offering to let her go home for the day, which also gives you time to find out a bit more.

2. At this stage, there is no way you can tell whether Sandy's story is correct. There are many possibilities: Sandy's work may not be up to scratch; there may be personality difficulties; Mary may have an unfortunate management style; Sandy may be distressed by other things in her life which distort her perception; Sandy may be being vindictive. However, it is equally possible that what you have heard is true and that Mary is harassing Sandy. It is your responsibility to ensure that harassment doesn't take place.

3. If Sandy or anyone else comes to you in confidence, respect that. However, if Sandy wishes you to do anything about

the harassment, then you are inhibited (but not thwarted) if she doesn't want Mary to know she has talked to you. In some harassment situations, the complainant may be afraid of the alleged harasser; this is real, and their feelings should be respected. If you have been asked not to divulge confidences, then you still have an obligation to do something (you have been made aware of the stressor) and the easiest way of addressing the issue then is to depersonalize it by raising the issue of harassment and the company policy (if you have one) with the whole team. If Sandy is happy for you to investigate her claim, then it is still incumbent on you to tell as few people as is necessary. This is vital both for Sandy and Mary's sakes.

4. The workplace issues are harassment, Sandy's possible ineffectiveness, supervisory practices or style, and reverberations on the whole team. The situation therefore needs to be addressed promptly and efficiently. To begin with, if Sandy has agreed, you need to talk to Mary to uncover her version of events. The outcome of this will determine what you do next and how wide your investigation needs to go. If Mary admits that there are problems and that she has had to raise relevant issues with Sandy, then you may need to discuss management style with Mary and keep the situation under close supervision, following it up with both parties. If, however, Mary denies that anything has happened, you may need to widen the investigation to the witnesses mentioned by Sandy. At this stage you should be trying to resolve the issues as informally as possible to avoid polarization and long-term effects.

5. If you have a company policy on this matter, it will probably set out recommended procedures for informal and formal resolutions of the issue. If there is no company policy, it will be assumed that you as manager are responsible for all such issues, and if Sandy wants to take formal action, she will have to use a more general grievance procedure.

6. If Sandy has had a number of days' sickness absence, this should have alerted you to some underlying problem.

Maybe your procedures for monitoring sickness, even informally, may need revising. Or perhaps Mary has been remiss in not reporting this to you. You might have been able to pick up the undercurrents long before Sandy comes to you in a distressed state.

7. Both parties to a case of harassment need support. If there is a company policy on harassment, it will probably have a built-in support system. If not, welfare officers or friends should be able to accompany the parties in any discussions surrounding a complaint. If Sandy is distressed, and has been weathering harassment for some time, she may well benefit from counselling, but it can only be an offer to her. If, in the course of investigation it is apparent that Mary is behaving in an unacceptable way, it could be that there are underlying reasons for this. It does not excuse the behaviour, but it might indicate Mary's need for additional support or counselling.

8. Documentation needs to be precise and confidential. Outcomes of meetings, witness statements or records of content need to be kept, with dates. Some harassment cases end as disciplinary matters; others may result in constructive dismissal claims or sexual or racial harassment complaints. For any future action, documents need to be well kept.

9. Reviewing the situation will depend on whether the matter has been resolved informally or formally. You as manager need to ensure that the team is working effectively and that any harassment has ceased. You will need to set up meetings with Sandy at regular intervals to monitor the success of your intervention. You may also seek regular meetings with Mary to check on procedures, supervision, etc. Formal resolutions usually have in-built review recommendations.

This case study raises many issues which go beyond the remit of this guide. The above discussion does not therefore seek to indicate how harassment cases should be investigated. Rather it draws attention to the complexity of such a complaint and the possible avenues for you to be aware of in deciding how to act.

I hope that the three case studies have allowed you to explore the practicalities of what has been raised elsewhere in the guide, and to underline that in your role as a manager you need to be sensitive to the many and varying aspects of people working together.

The following summary brings together, in a few short points, the essentials of effective management of distressed employees. It can serve as a reminder for the busy manager.

Summary

- Know your staff.
- Be sensitive to uncharacteristic changes in behaviour.
- Listen to your staff.
- Respect confidences.
- Reserve judgement.
- Offer support.
- Deal with issues immediately.
- Document essential details.
- Review any situation at regular intervals.
- Raise organizational 'deficiencies' at a senior level.

CHAPTER 10

Self-Help Measures for Managers and Employees

There is much that each one of us can do, without too much effort, both to reduce the amount of stress we experience and to protect ourselves from it. Whatever our situation, wherever we are in the workplace hierarchy, we can take effective action on behalf of our own health and wellbeing, and as a result improve our effectiveness at work.

The following suggestions and strategies can also be shared with your employees where you feel they may benefit from self-help. However, remember you can only *offer* such suggestions, as this book does. You mustn't expect that employees will necessarily take action because you, or I, think it best for them!

Personal strategies

Balancing our lives
Too few of us feel we have the balance of our lives right. We either have too much pressure or too little. We feel the choice has been taken away from us; we feel we cannot control the existence we have.

Regaining that balance is essential for our mental health. If we are spending all our waking hours at work and worrying about work, we have no quality time for ourselves or others in our lives. If life is all about working, what is the point of life? When are you going to benefit from the fruits of your labour, from the enjoyment of your hard-earned salary? Work for some of us is also pleasure, and is part of the fruit itself, but not for many.

So how do we regain the balance? We need to assume control of our whole lives. It's not happening to us: we are allowing it to happen. We *can* choose. We can choose to give ourselves time off, to take breaks, to have holidays, to go out for an evening, to spend Sunday in the park with the children, to climb mountains, to do nothing except contemplate the evening sky. An employer doesn't own you. And a good employer would not want you working for them twenty-four hours a day. They would know that it was not a good return on their investment.

Every one of us needs some work, some play; some stimulation, some relaxation. We owe it to ourselves, to our families, our friends and our employers to ensure that we have that balance. There is no reason at all for anyone to feel guilty at taking time for themselves. And if you have a demanding boss, read the section on work issues below.

Relaxation

There is a difference between relaxation and recreation, and we need to have both. Relaxation is a state of being mentally and/or physically at rest. Some of us have lost the ability to relax. Even when we are sitting in a soft armchair, our minds are racing away, our legs are twitching, and we want to get up and do something. Relaxation is a technique that has to be re-learned in adulthood, and re-learning may take time and patience. But it is one of the best ways of ensuring that you reduce the effects of stress, and for protecting yourself.

Have you ever felt your heart pounding before an interview, in a traffic jam, after an argument, or even when you thought you were doing nothing? Have you ever felt shortness of breath, or a vice-like band across your chest? A short relaxation exercise can counteract what is happening to you. It has the effect of slowing your heart rate and thus reducing the pounding, the fear, the excitement, the panic, the anxiety you may be experiencing.

This quick exercise can be done almost anywhere: in the car, in front of your boss, sitting in a comfortable armchair, waiting outside an interview room or lying in a warm bed waiting for sleep:

Relax your shoulders; take a deep breath, and then release it very slowly. Do this three times. In this time, your heart rate will have slowed down significantly.

A longer relaxation exercise of ten to twenty minutes regularly every day will help to minimize the detrimental effects of the pressures of everyday life. If you relax before you sleep, your body will be more alert and responsive when you awake. You'll feel better able to cope with the stresses of the day. There are numerous tapes on the market which help with relaxation. Some of these show you how to relax each muscle of your body in turn so that you are physically as relaxed as possible; others take it further to allow you to deal with specific problems you might have (eg sleeplessness, feeling overweight, low self-esteem). Choose a tape which suits your needs and your voice preferences. Most good bookshops will have a range of such cassettes, and even your public library may have them for loan.

Recreation

Having some form of recreational activity helps ensure that there is some balance in your life between home and work; between pressures and enjoyment. It does not matter what form of recreation you choose, as long as you get satisfaction and enjoyment from it. So whether you're a secret cordon bleu cook, or a stamp collector, an avid reader or a gardener, it doesn't matter. If you get fun and laughter from it, meet people and do exercise, then this is a bonus for your wellbeing.

But even a solitary, sedentary hobby has value, if you get pleasure from it.

When the form of recreation you choose starts to become another pressure on you, as some people find, then that is the time to change your activity. If your bowls partner becomes too competitive, or the political party makes unreasonable demands on your time, when the scouts and cubs start to irritate you, or the beer-making turns into another disaster which you can't laugh about, the activity has ceased to be recreational. Choose something else.

Exercise

We all know exercise is healthy for us. Too bad that we would rather spend our time in front of the television or propping up a bar! But to be good for us, exercise doesn't mean racing around a football pitch with twenty-one other zealots, or competing to get the first coronary on the squash court. Simply walking briskly instead of taking the car, walking up the stairs instead of waiting for a lift, can provide some exercise.

Exercise is beneficial for several reasons. Besides keeping our bodies in trim so that the vital organs are not overworked, exercise can be pleasurable (when we exercise, chemicals (endorphins) are released which make us feel good); it can occupy our minds, deflecting our attention from those worrying work issues; it can be a good social activity, allowing us to form new friendships, or to work in a supportive team; most of all, it can help reduce the negative effects of tension that build up when we have found ourselves in a stressful situation. Exercising regularly will ensure that the fight or flight responses mentioned earlier are dealt with physically. But if you are loath to exercise regularly, even a brisk walk round the block or a walk up a flight of stairs after you have been in a stressful situation will help reduce the levels of adrenalin in your body and lessen the uncomfortable symptoms you may be experiencing.

Healthy living

Even the words are a turn-off! But a balanced diet, sensible alcohol intake and no smoking are what your body craves, even if your mind tells you differently. In terms of stress, if your body is in a physical state of equilibrium, you will be able to cope with the pressures of life more easily, with fewer of the detrimental effects. Abuse your body and it will not support you when you are under pressure. Feeling guilty about what you eat or drink or smoke will only add to that pressure. Decide what is right for you, and go for it. Being lectured at is counter-productive, as we all know, whichever side we are on. If you want to change your lifestyle but feel you don't have the willpower, you could try hypnotherapy.

Sharing problems

Talking about issues or unpleasant experiences which are worrying you is cathartic. There are few of us who don't benefit from talking to someone else and sharing our problems. The difficulty is in finding someone to share with who doesn't then burden you with their own problems: the 'oh, that happened to me, too' syndrome. Sometimes, it's helpful to know that you're not alone. At other times, particularly when something has just happened to upset you, you cannot cope with hearing other people's experiences on top of your own. A supportive partner or friend, a relative or colleague may fulfil your needs. But if you haven't got anyone you are close to, or if you feel uncomfortable opening up to people you know, then maybe a counsellor could help. The British Association for Counselling can provide you with a list of accredited counsellors.

Bottling up your worries is unhelpful, and can lead to long-term health problems. A good cry is therapeutic, and tears are now thought to have a healing capacity. It's okay for anyone to cry: the macho, stiff upper lip is an unhealthy response to excessive pressures. If *you* cannot let go and release the tension you are feeling, how can you help your staff to do the same? If you are there for them, who is there for you? Make sure you have someone to support you.

Laughter

Just as tears are thought to have healing properties, so laughing and smiling are more than just a bit of fun. The act of smiling and laughing releases chemicals which actually make you feel better. So, treat yourself to a good laugh on a regular basis; make a collection of funny videos or cartoons or whatever you find amusing, so that when you are feeling low and miserable, you have some ready-made medicine to make you feel better. It really does work.

Sleep

There has always been controversy about the amount of sleep we each need. Some people seem to manage adequately on three or four hours a night, while others struggle with less than eight. But we all know that if we can't get to sleep at night, or if we wake in the early hours of the morning and can't get back to sleep, we worry about it. It's more likely to be the worry than the lack of sleep which adversely affects us the next day! Whatever the experts argue is the optimum amount of sleep, here are some useful tips if your sleep pattern is disrupted by the stresses you are under:

- Go easy on stimulants (tea, coffee, cola) in the evenings.
- Do something relaxing before you go to bed.
- Have a warm (not hot) relaxing bath before bed.
- Drink a cup of warm milk at bedtime or a herbal tea designed to aid sleep.
- Never go to bed straight after an argument or heated discussion – your mind will not be able to switch off.
- Don't work/study up to bedtime – always do a winding-down activity after you have spent an evening working.
- If you wake up worrying about something, or can't fall asleep because the day's events are going round and round in your mind, have a notepad by your bed and write down your worries. Then forget about them. They won't look as bad in the morning!
- If you can't fall asleep, don't lie there worrying about it. Get up and do something relaxing (listen to the radio, read a

book, do a relaxation exercise). When you feel relaxed, go back to bed and try again.

- If you wake early in the morning, again don't lie there worrying about the day ahead. Get up and do something pleasurable or indulgent. You will start work fresher despite the lack of sleep.
- Our bodies need regularity. Try to go to bed and get up at the same time each day, even weekends. The pattern will then take hold and you are less likely to wake at odd times.

Just resting your body physically and mentally will be more beneficial than tossing and turning in anguish at not being able to sleep. If you are sleeping badly, make sure you give yourself time for some rest.

Monitor yourself
Our lives seem to be so busy, there is rarely any time for ourselves. Yet if we don't give ourselves any time, we may not be aware when we are slipping into a downward spiral of dysfunction. Just as you need to be aware of changes that are happening in the behaviour of your employees, so you need to assess where you are, what you are feeling. This may take only a few minutes, perhaps when you wake up or when you get home from work. If you don't know how you are feeling, how will you know when to take action for yourself?

All you need to do is to ask yourself a few questions:

- Am I feeling happy most of the time?
- Is work still providing me with satisfaction?
- Am I seeing enough of my children, my partner, my family?
- Do I have time for my friends?
- Am I getting a reasonable night's sleep?
- Am I in good health?
- Am I drinking, eating, smoking too much?
- Are others complaining of my irritability?
- Am I enjoying my life?

If any of these areas causes you to stop and wonder, try analysing what is getting in the way and take action to rectify the situation. If necessary, take professional advice. Most of the solutions lie in your own hands; the hardest part is accepting that something is not right.

Challenge negative thinking

Each of us is bombarded by the negative thoughts and feelings of others around us: newspapers and television; our family; our managers; our employees; sales forecasts; grant reductions – the list is endless. But it is our own thoughts and feelings that are most destructive! We hold on to the negative thoughts that come into our heads, and let the positives fly away. If someone says something good about you and then your own manager throws your report back at you, which do you tell your partner about when you get home? Invariably it's the negative words. And we don't need other people to supply those for us: we're very good at being hard on ourselves when we've done something wrong, made a mistake, forgotten something, spoken out of turn ...

All negative thoughts, ours and other people's, make us feel much worse about things. It is the negative thoughts which seem to be going round and round in our minds when we're trying to sleep, or while we're eating our dinner. The only beneficiaries are the makers of sleeping pills or indigestion tablets! If we dismiss the negatives, if we give them no space in our thoughts, they will disappear, and we will feel more relaxed, more contented. Talk positively to yourself and to others and you will feel better about life.

Workplace strategies

Be assertive

One of the major problems for managers is that their staff do not tell them when things are not right. And the same applies to your managers if you keep quiet. If you are being expected to meet unreasonable deadlines, if your family life is suffering because you have to work late every night, if you do not have enough staff to delegate work to, tell your manager clearly and calmly. If you continue to take on extra pressures, to work excessive hours, your health will deteriorate and your efficiency will decrease. This is not good news for *your* manager. A good manager will listen and take action. A poor manager will cost the company dearly for ignoring your health. Once you or your staff have raised such issues, the manager has a legal responsibility to do something.

If you have to make the choice between your health and your job, which is more important? Can you maintain your family or your mortgage better in good health or in poor health? The choice can only be yours.

Take breaks

Left to your own devices at home, don't you give yourself a break when you've been gardening or decorating or whatever task you are doing? And if you don't, do you notice that what started as a pleasurable activity becomes a chore, or you start making little errors and become irritated with yourself? The same applies to the work situation. Our concentration spans are limited, and if we don't take regular breaks, our efficiency falls. The longer we work at something non-stop, the larger the drop in efficiency. Taking regular breaks gives us the ability to recover our original enthusiasm or energy for a task.

Breaks also serve to relieve the tension when things are not going right for us. For example, if we are trying to write a report and get writer's block, a break perhaps in the form of making a cup of tea, or a walk down the corridor or engaging in a totally different work task may help us to release our creativity.

The same applies to the necessity of taking a reasonable length of lunch break. No one will give you brownie points for being so dedicated. They are more likely to realize you are a mug and treat you accordingly!

Taking holidays

We are provided with annual leave because organizations are aware that their employees cannot keep going forever without a change of scenery, a long break from the work situation.

Those of you who feel that you are indispensable to the company and cannot therefore take a holiday are doing no one, least of all yourselves or your company, a favour. Take your holiday every year, the full amount, and you will come back to work refreshed and with your energy replenished. Taking your annual leave in the form of one- or two-day breaks at a time may not provide the total break you need from the work situation.

And while you're on holiday, leave the mobile telephone behind. It is not a break if your company contacts you at every crisis. Remember, if you were hospitalized following a stress-induced heart attack, the company would find someone else to help them in the crisis period. No one is indispensable.

Manage your time effectively

A whole industry has been built up in time management training. While many of us legitimately feel we have too much work, too much pressure on us, some of us could use our time more effectively, thus reducing the pressure on us. Some of the key issues we need to address are:

- setting goals;
- prioritizing work according to these goals;
- learning to let go and delegate more;
- not procrastinating – that just means that we deal with the same pieces of paper every day and achieve nothing but worry!
- using the waste-paper basket more!
- seeking help from colleagues or our manager.

If you know you have problems in any of the areas above, get yourself on a time management training course.

Reward your successes

In the work situation, it is rare that we are praised for what we achieve. It is expected of us. And yet, just as your employees would feel valued and more committed if you praised or thanked them, so would you benefit from positive strokes from your own manager.